one-STAR REVIEWS

THE VERY BEST REVIEWS 👍
OF THE VERY WORST PRODUCTS

C. Coville

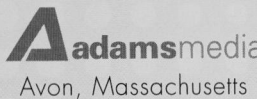

Aadamsmedia
Avon, Massachusetts

Published by
Adams Media, a division of F+W Media, Inc.
57 Littlefield Street, Avon, MA 02322. U.S.A.
www.adamsmedia.com

ISBN 10: 1-4405-7908-3
ISBN 13: 978-1-4405-7908-0
eISBN 10: 1-4405-7909-1
eISBN 13: 978-1-4405-7909-7

Printed in the United States of America.

10 9 8 7 6 5 4 3 2 1

Many of the designations used by manufacturers and sellers to distinguish their products are claimed as trademarks. Where those designations appear in this book and F+W Media, Inc. was aware of a trademark claim, the designations have been printed with initial capital letters.

Photo credits provided at the back of the book.

Cover design by Sylvia McArdle.
Cover images © Anan Kaewkhammul, dipressionist,
Monika Adamczyk/123RF; *www.hookedontoys.com/productdetails.aspx?Item
ID=3270&ParentCatID=194.*

This book is available at quantity discounts for bulk purchases.
For information, please call 1-800-289-0963.

DEDICATION

For Marceline

CONTENTS

PART II: Terrible Stuff

INTRODUCTION

Welcome to the dark, slimy underbelly of life on this product-consuming planet of ours. Here you will find hundreds of one-star-worthy items and establishments as well as consumers who demand craftsman-level quality from a 39-cent product (that's with shipping included). There may come a time when you ask yourself, *"What on earth were these people thinking?"* But just know that eight out of ten customers agree that these reviews are comedic gems, so be sure to read on.

Culled from the swamps of largely unmoderated ratings sites like Amazon, Walmart.com, Yelp, and Goodreads, each entry gives you an honest—or at least hilariously pungent—picture of the product or venue at hand. From scathing reviews about exploding alarm systems to appalling tales of restaurants that serve each dish with a side of unidentifiable teeth, these consumers' candid thoughts are truly masterpieces in their own right. Sure, we've all stupidly ordered the wrong product or have accidentally eaten in a less-than-sanitary restaurant at least once, but these frank assessments go beyond everyday disappointment. *Way beyond.*

Filled with heartbreak, outrage, and sheer insanity, this ridiculous collection includes only the best critiques the Internet has to offer, so brace yourself as these one-of-a-kind reviewers unleash the snark!

PART I

TERRIBLE REVIEWS

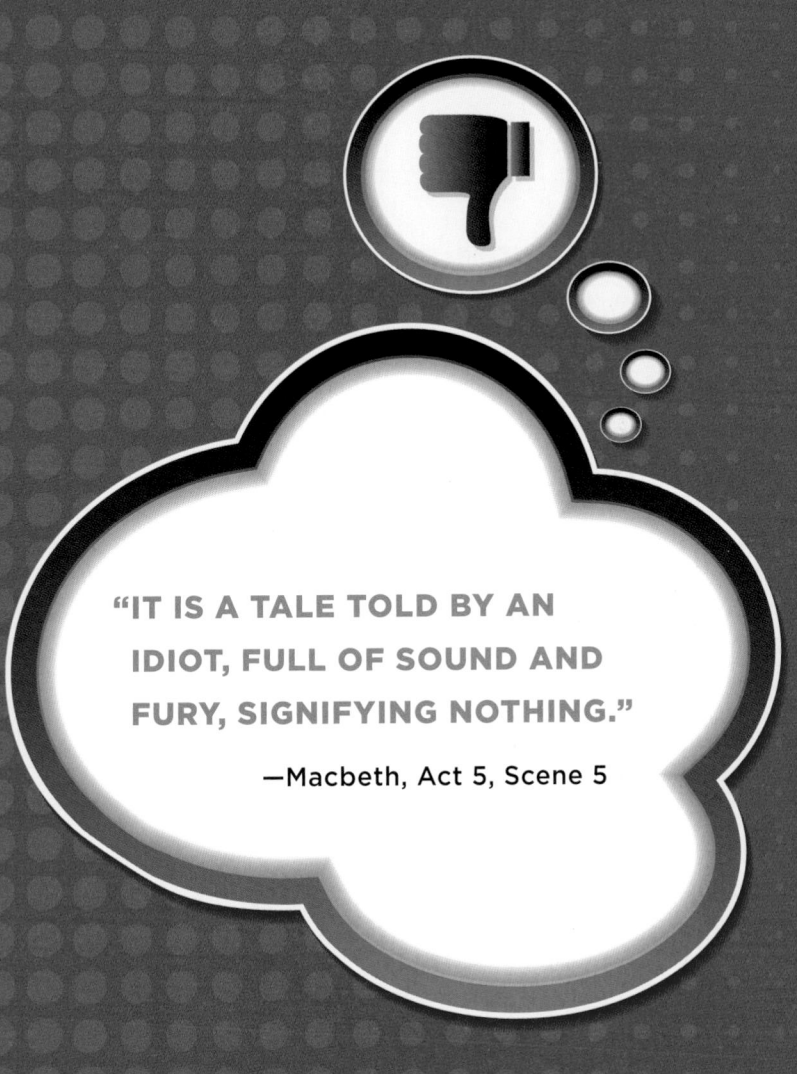

"IT IS A TALE TOLD BY AN IDIOT, FULL OF SOUND AND FURY, SIGNIFYING NOTHING."

—Macbeth, Act 5, Scene 5

Chapter 1

YOU'RE DOING IT WRONG

These reviewers did not use the products they bought as God—or the manufacturer—intended. Or maybe they just didn't read the fine print, or *any print at all*, so they went in expecting something that a product couldn't offer. Or maybe the products these people were expecting exist only in their heads, alongside self-milking cows, cats that don't poop, and speakers that never make that annoying buzzing sound when you put your phone next to them. Whatever the cause, when things went wrong, no one considered the fact that it might be their fault. Nope, instead they decided to hammer out a good one-star review.

THE PRODUCT: Last Supper Poster Print by Ron Jenkins

![Last Supper Poster Print]

THE REVIEW: "didn't realize it was african american, wanted reg . . . want to return both posters."

Come on, lady. Jesus's message was intended for all the races of man, whether black, Asian, or "regular."

★☆☆☆☆

THE PRODUCT: Niagara Parks Butterfly Conservatory, Niagara Falls, Canada

THE REVIEW: "Only go if you like butterflies"

"Butterfly Conservatory did not feature a single waterslide, high-end electronics boutique, or Japanese sword-fighting display."

THE PRODUCT: *Mermaids: The Body Found*, Animal Planet, 2012

THE REVIEW: "I just wanted to believe in mermaids, was that too much too ask?!"

And I want to believe that all puppies live forever, but you don't see me giving bad reviews to pet cemeteries. Well, except to Breezy Pines Pet Graveyard in San Francisco, but that's because they wouldn't allow my dog and cat to be buried together. Said it was "unnatural." Anyway, mermaids aren't real.

THE PRODUCT: Easy Chocolate Mousse, Three Ways Recipe

THE REVIEW: "I didn't try this recipe, but anything including cool whip scares me. I do have a solution, a recipe that is just as easy and probably much better than the fake taste that comes along with cool whip. silken tofu- one package good quality, semi-sweet chocolate 70% cocoa (or more if you're a fan of dark), melted over a double boiler, roughly 300-350 grams put the tofu in a food processor until smooth, add the melted chocolate and run until chocolate is incorporated, you may add vanilla if you wish. put in serving cups/bowls and refrigerate until set delicious! trust me the tofu does not make it weird or gross"

Yes, this alternate recipe is "just as easy" as dumping in some damn Cool Whip. Just leave us to eat our hydrogenated vegetable oil sweetened with high fructose corn syrup in shameful peace, all right?

THE PRODUCT: Tender Greens Restaurant, West Hollywood, CA

THE REVIEW: "Feeding food to animals that are killed is not sustainable. And certainly not TENDER OR GREEN!!"

Never put the word "green" in your restaurant name, or you'll anger reviewers who believe all meat-serving restaurants must display the word "murder" and at least one diagram of a baby cow being strangled to death. Also, never feed food to animals that are killed. It just falls right back out of their mouth, and then Killed Animal CSI gets mad at you for getting hay all over the murder scene.

★☆☆☆☆

THE PRODUCT: AntWorks Illuminated Combo Ant Farm

THE REVIEW: "All the ants we gathered have died within 2 days. I have collected more ants with the same results two additional times."

The ant farm this reviewer is talking about is designed for a particular species of ant that must be purchased with the farm as an entire colony. The fact that she "gathered" random, doomed individual ants instead makes her an ant serial killer, or maybe an ant alien-abductor that ants tell stories about around their little ant campfires.

THE PRODUCT: *Crafting with Cat Hair: Cute Handicrafts to Make with Your Cat,* by Kaori Tsutaya

CRAFTING WITH CAT HAIR
Cute Handicrafts to Make with Your Cat

by Kaori Tsutaya
translated from the Japanese
by Amy Hirschman

THE REVIEW: "It made me think you could craft bags and things, when in reality all it shows you how to craft are SMALL items to apply to your bag or SMALL pictures."

He has been raiding old ladies' homes for YEARS to get enough cat fur to make a suit to wear to the office every day so that he can take revenge on his annoying coworker who has a cat allergy. And this book turned out to be USELESS.

★★★★★

THE PRODUCT: Holy Bible: Precious Moments, Pink

THE REVIEW: "i am disappointed with the bible. . . . the whole point was to get a king james bible and this clearly is not. what a waste of my money."

It's just not right when pink Precious Moments Bibles don't feature the somber linguistic grandeur of the seventeenth-century King James translation. It's like they're not taking religion seriously.

THE PRODUCT: Cuisinart SmartStick Extendable Shaft Hand Blender

THE REVIEW: "I struggled to control [the handheld blender] while pulled it into the glass held between my legs. . . the blender slipped from my hands and began spinning wildly in my lap. I reached to grab it and turn it off, but it sliced my thumb, and then I punched it onto the floor, where it spun and spun."

If your handheld appliance features razor-sharp spinning blades, the best way to test it is by thrusting it downward between your legs. The key is to drink a few six-packs beforehand, so you're not too nervous, and maybe suspend some live wires and angry rattlesnakes at head level just in case.

★★★★★

THE PRODUCT: Blueberry Muffins Recipe

THE REVIEW: "I subsituted the oil for applesauce and they turned out horrible."

"Also substituted ball bearings for blueberries. Results not popular at church picnic."

Chapter 2

WHaT DID YOU expect?

"You get what you pay for." Most of us learned this as children when we begged our parents to buy us an Optimus Prime toy from the Rite-Aid discount aisle and then accidentally pulled his head off three minutes later. Unfortunately, it seems like other people somehow missed out on Optimus's solemn life lesson. Here's to the people who purchase a 99-cent, plastic novelty mustache and then are shocked to realize that it wasn't handcrafted by a hipster collective in Brooklyn.

★☆☆☆☆

THE PRODUCT: HDE Prankster Shock Gag Grenade

THE REVIEW: "Unbelievably strong shock. It looked like my son got tased. This is an ADULT prank - not for kids of any age."

And now you've set this man's son up for a lifetime of believing that grenades are objects to be feared, instead of hugged and cherished. Great work, guys.

THE PRODUCT: The Violet Hour Lounge, Chicago, IL

THE REVIEW: "My hot sister and 2 hot girlfriends waited in line for 2 hours to have a drink. . . . Why did we wait?"

Calling your sister "hot" in a Yelp review, and then wondering why the bouncer didn't think you were classy enough to skip the line: all in a day's work for this reviewer. Maybe it was that weird, twelve-fingered baby he was holding.

★☆☆☆☆

THE PRODUCT: America Star Books (previously "PublishAmerica")

THE REVIEW: "This is not a good company to turn your manuscript over. It sounds good when you hear 'FREE', but don't be fooled by these people because while you do business with them, your book will only be sold to yourself, family and friends."

You should be happy with that, author. Almost none of my family or friends bought my self-published book, The Girl Who Fought Cute Vampires and Was Also Good at Sports.

★☆☆☆☆

THE PRODUCT: Viral Media Enterprises

THE REVIEW: "FANMENOW got me the thousands of followers and then after a few months- they all are gone !! What a bunch of scam artist f&cks !"

This guy paid a company to scam people into believing he had more Twitter followers than he really did, and then got all pink with rage when the company scammed him. With that level of self-awareness, all he needs is a varsity jacket and some douchey hair and he can find work as the guy who gets punched at the end of a teen movie.

THE PRODUCT: "As Seen On TV" Perfect Bacon Bowl

THE REVIEW: "'bowl' didnt stay together,burned my fingers with the bacon grease."

"Should have come with bacon oven mitts."

★☆☆☆☆

THE PRODUCT:
Fatima's Psychic Studio, Salem, MA

THE REVIEW: "When I came along this place I thought the big sign saying psychic seemed pretty legit. I was wrong."

If there's one thing trustworthier than a psychic, it's a psychic with a big neon sign that says "PSYCHIC." There are laws covering that stuff, kind of like how undercover cops have to tell you they're cops if you ask them.

THE PRODUCT: Mrs Austin Psychic Advisor, Charlotte, NC

THE REVIEW: "She had me go buy window cleaner furniture polish and spray paint saying she used the chemicals in the products to use in your case. I believe she just needed those things to clean her house."

Interesting fact: Japanese mythology features a mischievous spirit called an akaname *that lives in bathrooms and licks up mold and human waste. Another interesting fact: this psychic is currently fighting one.*

THE PRODUCT: The Argyle Oracle, Sydney, Australia

THE REVIEW: "They just sat there and insulted me and my boyfriend and said I don't belong in their country."

On the plus side, Racist Psychics *would make a good reality TV show.*

★☆☆☆☆

THE PRODUCT: LookRichForLess.com

THE REVIEW: "I have ordered a replica watch from lookrichforless.com . . . a Bvlgari Aluminum Granite Dial Rubber Band II . . . . When i opened the package the watch was not seal or wrapped. After wearing the watch for almost two weeks the band broke. When i called lookrichforless.com and . . . I asked for my money back he said your funny and hung up."

Many of us long for those honest, pre-Internet days when you bought your cheap replica watches from a shady guy on the beach, who then packed up his stuff and ran away while you were distracted by seagulls.

THE PRODUCT: Hasbro Ouija Board Game

THE REVIEW: "this doesn't work at alll think it was a waste of money I tryed it so many times NOTHING shacking my head . . .im so mad . . .I really thought it wud work but notttt< idk if u want u can buy it .mayb u have luck but I wudnt bye another EVER AGAIN"

Wait, wait, we're finally getting something from the spirit world: "USE . . . A . . . SPELLCHECKER."

★☆☆☆☆

THE PRODUCT: Design Toscano Good Dog Gone Bad Peeing Bulldog Figurine

THE REVIEW: "love it, it's cute and I got a lot of compliments, however for the price it was too small. Should of came with fire hydedrint."

"Even if your statue of a peeing bulldog already attracts lots of compliments, don't be afraid to demand more. Follow your dreams and ask the universe to bring you that extra urine-soaked fire hydedrint."
—Customer who also purchased The Secret

THE PRODUCT: Organism Pen Holder Sexy Ass Bum Butt Girl Toy Novelty Funny Gift Joke Present

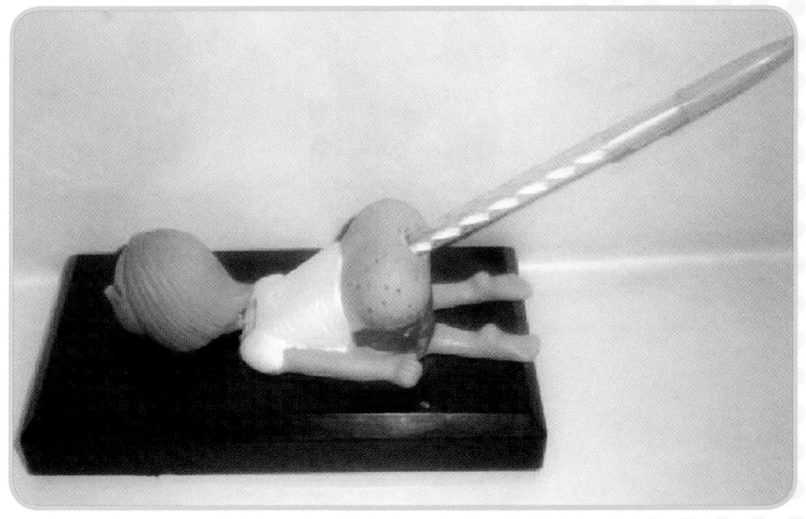

THE REVIEW: "My wife bought this for me as a gag gift. I hate it for so many reasons. it came from china in styro-foam wrapped in tape. (worried about cancer)"

It's sad when novelty pen holders shaped like ladies' butts aren't up to the standard that men of quality have come to expect. But really, this reviewer should be less worried about cancer and more worried about the message his wife is sending when she presents him with a pen-penetrated butt figurine.

★★★★★

THE PRODUCT: *If You Want Closure in Your Relationship Start with Your Legs: A Woman's Guide to Understanding Men*, by Big Boom

A GUIDE TO UNDERSTANDING MEN
If You Want Closure in Your Relationship, Start with Your Legs
BIG BOOM

THE REVIEW: "When I bought this book my hope was that it was written according to God's word. There was very little that really gives God glory."

Other things this reviewer rated one star for not containing expected amount of God's glory: local "Starbutts" strip club, the Church of Satan, and Wall Street.

THE PRODUCT: *Dinosaur Wars: Earthfall*, by Thomas Hopp

THE REVIEW: "I just couldn't get behind the idea of alien dinosaurs coming to wipe out earth . . . ."

"When I picked up Dinosaur Wars, *I was expecting a grimly realistic homosexual love triangle set in 1920s Berlin."*

★★★★★

THE PRODUCT: *Amish Vampires in Space*, by Kerry Nietz

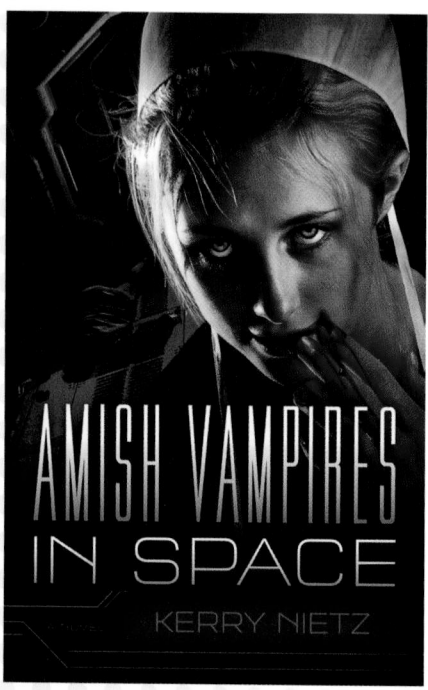

THE REVIEW: "This book had lackluster characters that I could have cared LESS about from page one."

Ugh, I hate it when they make the Amish space vampires two-dimensional. I want a real sense of what went on in their minds and backgrounds to make them become Amish space vampires. Not flat portrayals that are exactly the same as every other Amish space vampire character out there.

THE PRODUCT: Pack of 6 White Decorative Ceramic Accent Balls 3.5"

THE REVIEW: "They have a fairly small hole in them, but worse is that there are 4 'teeth' marks that symmetrically surround the hole where the ball is probably gripped during the manufacturing process. The price would be great if these were decent balls, but they are not."

It sucks when you pay a great price and then your balls end up having teeth marks on them.

★★★★★

THE PRODUCT: Fire Dragon Figure

THE REVIEW: "Make believe. Just wasn't very exciting and EXTREMELY overpriced!"

Is it too much to ask for someone to ship this man a real goddamn dragon?

Chapter 3

WHAT DID YOU EXPECT? DATING EDITION

You'll be shocked to learn that sites offering hundreds of attractive and lonely "singles in your area" are not always telling the truth. Hell, it turns out that those anonymous hot babes and male models who profess their love thirty minutes into the relationship and then ask for your credit card information *might not be trustworthy*. I know, I'm shaking and crying, too. Luckily, there are a bunch of reviews out there to warn us before we whip out our money orders in service of the next handsome Nigerian prince who catches our eye.

THE PRODUCT: Fuckbook.com

THE REVIEW: "I signed up for a fuckbook account and after a minute of looking around I found out that I cannot read messages unless I am a premium user which means that I should pay money to become premium user . . . . It does not value you as a customer."

It just stabs me right in the clavicle that the people behind "fuckbook .com" do not have a genuine, almost spiritual desire to connect men with decent partners they can grow old with.

★★★★★

THE PRODUCT: JustHookUp.com

THE REVIEW: "Enter a zip code where 50 people live in 500 miles and they will convince you that 200 horney women, all wanting you, live within 5 minutes of you."

You mean the forest around my house is NOT filled with sexy woodland dryads looking for hot, leafy hookups?

★★★★★

THE PRODUCT: Milfaholic.com

THE REVIEW: "I wrote back to all girls asking them to put a chocolate-vanilla ice cream in their right hand and a pepsi on the other and send this back to me to make me believe that they were actually real people . . . not one reply has arrived . . . ."

I guess this means that either the profiles on the site are fake, or that you mixed up Milfaholic.com with Ihaveanicecreamandpepsiwebcamfetish .com.

★★★★★

THE PRODUCT: Jaguars Club, El Paso, TX

THE REVIEW: "Halfway through this private dance when she began to rub on me I informed her this would do her no good, as I had prostate cancer and I could no longe get sexually excited. She continued anyway."

So it turns out that some people really do go to strip clubs for the conversation, and they just haven't been able to admit it this whole time due to the pressures of the male role exerted on them by our patriarchal society. Or maybe they just really love glitter, and don't realize that you can also purchase it at a craft store.

THE PRODUCT: ChnLove.com

THE REVIEW: "If chnlove.com won't allow me to communicate with these genuine women after you have already scammed me out of hundreds of dollars using fake profiles and dishonest translators, then I demand that all my money be returned to me. Its bad enough that I have been scammed out of so much money already, but to deny me access to the genuine ladies is an even bigger insult."

In other words, he thinks the shady overseas dating site is brimming with attractive ladies who want nothing more than to sprint in his direction while tearing off their clothes, but they are being held in check by the cruel site owners. Some people never learn . . . .

THE PRODUCT: Anastasia.com

THE REVIEW: "when my wife divorced me because she did not need me anymore for her permission to stay in my country i was very happy when one day i discovered anastasia.com on my computer."

Yep, some people really never learn.

★☆☆☆☆

THE PRODUCT: eHarmony

THE REVIEW: "ive been on eharmony for over three months and havent met a single person who responds with interest . . . is there really any enjoyment from a loveless existence i think not, human beings are social creatures being alone is like that of the wolf, immediate fear of death because people cannot survive alone."

Dude, Tom Hanks survived alone on that deserted island for years. Get yourself a decorated soccer ball and put a nice wig on it. No, not that mop head, a real wig . . . . Have some pride for god's sake.

★☆☆☆☆

THE PRODUCT: Milfaholic.com

THE REVIEW: "I've sent out over 30 messages and have not received any back from the supposedly horny hot babes on this site I have noticed a lot of these babes are from the same small town (near me) of less than 500 population there were more women on this site from this town then there are people in that town"

"I immediately got in my car and drove there at 120 mph, realizing that I lived next to the best town in America."

★☆☆☆☆

THE PRODUCT: Dream-Marriage.com

THE REVIEW: "Who wants a Ukranian $#*! anyway? Did anyone forget the cold war?"

We laugh now, but after thirty years of wedded bliss with my own Russian bride, I noticed a beige, putty-like substance that appeared to be hiding something on her upper lip. I ripped it off and . . . yup, you guessed it. Joseph Stalin.

★☆☆☆☆

THE PRODUCT: U.S. Army, Kabul, Afghanistan

THE REVIEW: "i have been contacted on many occasions by us army personnel asking for money to get them out of the army in afghanistan. it makes the army look as though they do not look after their personnel . . . . these people should be stopped from being allowed to contact women . . . ."

After this, she contacted the government of Nigeria and asked them to take care of their royal family better, so that their princes will stop asking her for money. She then wrote long emails to several family members with hacked Twitter accounts asking why they were suddenly so passionate about having bigger penises.

★☆☆☆☆

THE PRODUCT: MillionaireDates.com

THE REVIEW: "One day I get this message from this man that is supposable in the Army stationed at an Army base in Nigeria . . . . He said he was from IL . . . . He needed to transfer his money which the government had in a special account for him and open up a bank account here in the states. so he asked me if I could help him with that and I said yes I don't see why not."

It's very sad that this lady was scammed by a guy pretending to be in the military, but didn't she think to question why someone earning a U.S. military wage would be on a site called "Millionaire Dates"? Half of those guys qualify for food stamps. What, he stole a $30 million fighter jet and hid it in his garage?

★☆☆☆☆

THE PRODUCT: MillionaireDates.com

THE REVIEW: "there are So many FAKE MILLIONAIRES at that site."

Oh. I guess that explains why someone earning a U.S. military wage would be there.

★★★★★

THE PRODUCT: Fatty Patty Blow Up Doll

THE REVIEW: "I purchased Fatty Patty as a surprise Birthday present for a friend. He was thrilled but I wasn't . . . . This doll could fit in my own swim suit and before you think I must be large . . . I wear size 4! . . . granted her breasts are extremely large but everything else is small. I WANTED A FAT BLOW UP DOLL!!!!"

Did you try blowing her up a bit more?

Chapter 4
NOT THEIR FAULT

not long ago, it was common for deranged Amazon readers to give one-star reviews to eBooks because they didn't approve of the price set by the publisher, as if that were the poor author's fault. But the reviews in this chapter are somehow even worse than that. Take a look at some of the *weirdest* reasons that people think the product they purchased deserves a one-star review.

★☆☆☆☆

THE PRODUCT: *Laptops for Seniors for Dummies*, by Nancy C. Muir

THE REVIEW: "Item was returned. Bought an iPad 2 instead of a laptop."

"Book failed to morph accordingly."

THE PRODUCT: The Godfather Collection: The Coppola Restoration (Blu-ray)

THE REVIEW: "I returned the product. Did not view. Another family member had the product and had recently bought a similar product and so there was no necessity for me to keep it"

DVDs have a sentry alarm designed to go off and stop you from buying a copy when your family already owns one. Sadly, this one's microchip was missing because of a factory coup in China.

⭐⭐⭐⭐⭐

THE PRODUCT: *Les Misérables* (Kindle Edition)

THE REVIEW: "I DID NOT BUY THIS BOOK!!!!!!!!!!! I DON'T HAVE A CLUE WHAT YOU ARE ASKING OF ME. I WILL NOT SPEND MONEY ON THIS BOOK AND AT THE SAME TIME IF YOU SEND IT TO ME, I WILL RETURN IT TO YOU RTS!!!"

Another victim of the dark-suited government operatives that break into private citizens' homes and download Les Misérables *onto their Kindles. When will America be free of the tentacle-grasp of Big French Literature?!*

THE PRODUCT: *The Lord of the Rings,* by J.R.R. Tolkien

THE REVIEW: "Is it the next book after the hobbot? How mant pages?"

You're thinking of Tolkien's lesser-known later work, Hobbot: Rise of the Shiredroids.

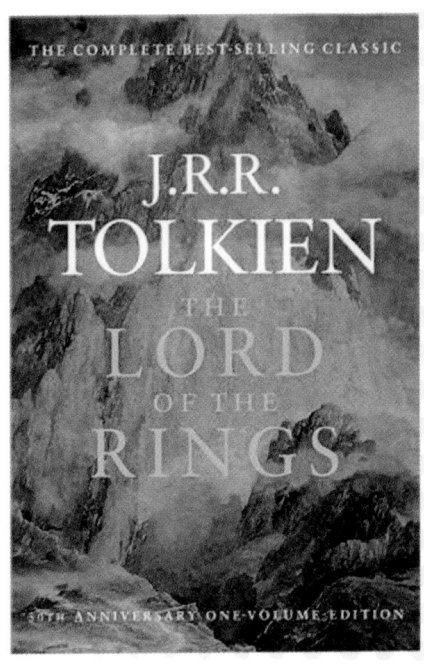

★★★★★

THE PRODUCT: Paschall Truck Lines, Inc.

THE REVIEW: "Paschall is the Hebrew word for the Passover lamb in the Old Testament. Thus the Old Testament mantra that all other races are 'dogs' i.e. male pagan temple prostitues/ homsexuals! Thus lies and deceit and all manner of evil is perfectly ok with all segments of Paschall Truck Lines operations . . . ."

And truck *comes from the Latin word* trochus *meaning "iron wheel," and it turns out Latin was spoken by the Romans. So if you think about it, Paschall Truck Lines must also be perfectly okay with* feeding innocent people to lions. *Just how deep does this rabbit hole go, Paschall?*

★☆☆☆☆

THE PRODUCT: Motel 6 Hollywood, Los Angeles, CA

THE REVIEW: "A friend of mine died in one of the rooms here in May . . . try to pick a place that at least doesn't feel like somebody died in your room."

This reviewer's story is sad, but she provides no other context. Did her friend die because the ceiling fan got loose and started flying around the room like a deadly toy helicopter, and now the reviewer wants to warn other people of this underappreciated danger? Or is she just worried about angry spirits messing around with the coffee maker while you're trying to sleep?

★☆☆☆☆

THE PRODUCT: CTA Digital Kitchen Knife Block with Adjustable View iPad Holder

THE REVIEW: "Will this also fit a Samsung Galaxy 10.1 tablet? You know, just in case we didn't all drink the iJunk Kool-Aid?"

Not long after this, the reviewer stormed out of a pet store, yelling something about them not selling Chevy Volts.

★ ☆ ☆ ☆ ☆

THE PRODUCT: Pow Gloves Hiro-Shaka Glove White

THE REVIEW: "MAY GOD LEAD US TO GLOVES THAT ARE PROPERLY ADVERTISED ESPECIALLY FOR THE PRICE THEY ATTEMPT TO SELL THEM FOR!"

God is busy taking the requests of kids with bone cancer. Try praying to Glovnor, the lesser-known Etruscan deity of hand garments.

★★★★★

THE PRODUCT: Hopscotch Technology BOB The Screentime Controller

THE REVIEW: "I think its the worst device ever. You take away childrens rights. It also is a scam! The people who make this device also make toys for kids to play outside with. All they want you to do is force your kids to play outside with the toys they make."

This review was definitely not written by a child sitting on another child's shoulders wearing a trench coat and hat.

THE PRODUCT: iRobot Roomba 550 Vacuum Cleaning Robot

THE REVIEW: "I was so fond of my Roomba I talked to it like it was my pet - now I feel as if my pet died and the company doesn't seem to give a hoot."

Be comforted. Your Roomba is in Roomba Valhalla now, fighting alongside Roomba Odin in preparation for Dust Bunny Ragnarök.

★★★★★

THE PRODUCT: "Tasty Tyrone" Inflatable Doll

THE REVIEW: "It wasnt tyrone"

"Detective," the woman sobbed as the FBI paranormal investigator surveyed the bloodied remains of the bachelorette party. "What came out of that box . . . it wasn't Tyrone."

THE PRODUCT: *Dr. Atkins' New Diet Revolution, Revised Edition*, by Robert C. Atkins, MD

THE REVIEW: "My wife lost the use of her legs and our cat is dead . . . . What kind of madness is this diet? It's bad karma from killing animals."

You know you weren't supposed to eat your wife's legs and your cat, right? Even if there was no other animal protein in the house and the grocery store didn't open until ten?

Copyrighted Material

COMPLETELY UPDATED!
The Must-Have NEW Edition

DR. ATKINS' *NEW* DIET REVOLUTION

- Expanded edition with new recipes, diet tips, and research
- Updated information on Atkins' safe, easy, and effective method for lasting weight-loss
- Over 250 weeks on the *New York Times* bestseller list

ROBERT C. ATKINS, M.D.

Copyrighted Material

★★★★★

THE PRODUCT: *Love* (German Edition), by Stephen King

THE REVIEW: "This book sucks, it is written in German, like the last three books I bought from Amazon.com. If I read German I might like it, but I don't, hence the reason for my opinion."

I hated Stephen King's "randomly writing in German" period, too. So pretentious, and he could never get the adjective declensions right.

THE PRODUCT: Sonic Alert SB1000 Sonic Boom Alarm Clock

THE REVIEW: "this was advertised as a vibrating alarm, but did not come with vibrator and seller could not provide vibrator."

Are you sure they couldn't provide it, or could the phone operators just not stop giggling long enough to get your address?

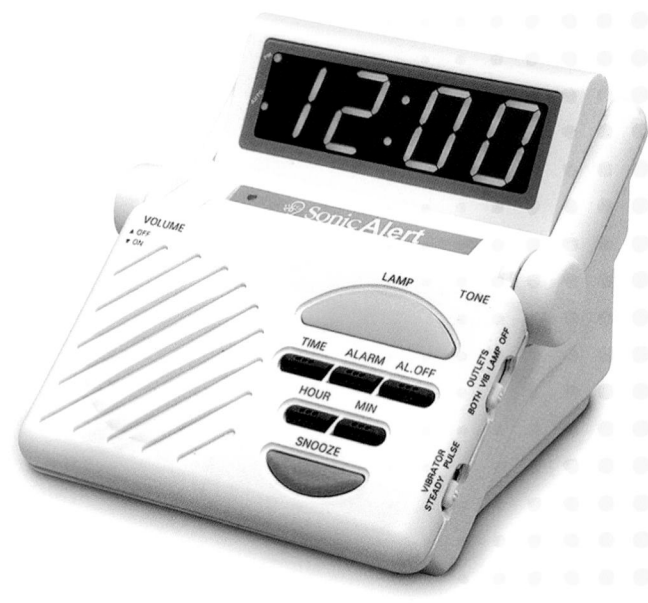

★★★★★

THE PRODUCT: McDreams Hotel, Wuppertal City, Germany

THE REVIEW: "this wass very very creepy hotel. there were some dead men souls and jinns living in the hotel. dont ever go there very very creepy."

Listen hater, those dead men's souls and jinn only wanted to get along and have a nice vacation, just like you. Next you'll be telling them they can't get married.

THE PRODUCT: My Size Darth Vader Figure

THE REVIEW: "My in-laws took my son to the toy store and my son picked this toy. It's extremely useless . . . . It simply stands there. It's a complete waste of money."

"Refuses to come to life despite literally dozens of telekinesis attempts and midi-chlorian blood transfusions. I am now reduced to Force-choking my own enemies, like some sort of Tatooine peasant."

Chapter 5
SUPER FANS AND CONTRARIANS

There are those books and movies that are basically the kittens of the entertainment world: inoffensive, agreeable, and almost universally loved. Some reviewers, though, don't agree. Let's call these guys Contrarians, because "kitten haters" is a bit strong. They're the people who don't see what the big deal is about *The Iliad*, or *The Lord of the Rings*, or whatever. And rather than simply shrugging it off as a difference in taste like a normal person would, they decide the other 98 percent of the population must simply be drowning in a swamp of wrongness.

If they can just *get the word out* by writing the right bad review, maybe everyone else on Earth will realize they've been deceived all these years, and that Shakespeare wasn't that great after all. I mean, the guy was English. That's almost like being French.

And then there's the flip side of these reviewers: the super-fans. These fans like a popular franchise. They like it *a lot*. And they will get very, *very* angry if a certain franchise-related product does not live up to their expectations. I'm talking *one-star* angry.

★★★★★

THE PRODUCT: *Frozen* (2013)

THE REVIEW: "For a woman who lives in a palace of ice, she doesn't seem to have put any kind of grip on her soles . . . ."

I do agree that the shoe issue really cut into the realism of Elsa's magical ice powers. And that dress would have gone much better with some sturdy snow boots.

★☆☆☆☆

THE PRODUCT: *The Lord of the Rings* Trilogy, by J.R.R. Tolkien

THE REVIEW: "I'm writing a chapter book like lord of the rings. It has wizards dwarves and stuff like that. It starts off with this greedy dwarf king whobfinds this stone and names in the adriel stone known for its beauty WHen the king looked into the stone he saw death because he was so greedy. He started aging quickly and crumbled to dust."

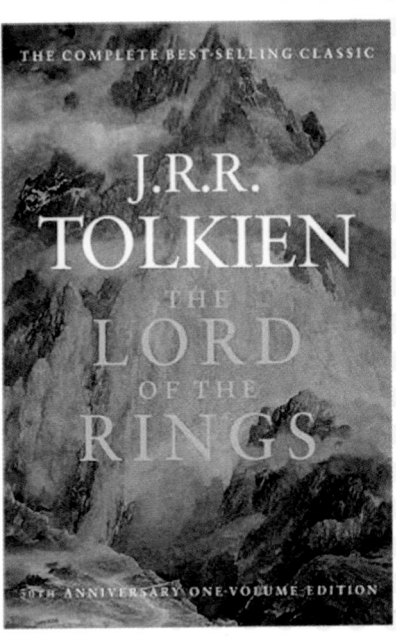

Geez, if you're going to write a bad review of The Lord of the Rings *because your own unpublished novel is better, at least put in a spoiler warning. I probably won't even read it now.*

★★★★★

THE PRODUCT: *The Fellowship of the Ring*, by J.R.R. Tolkien

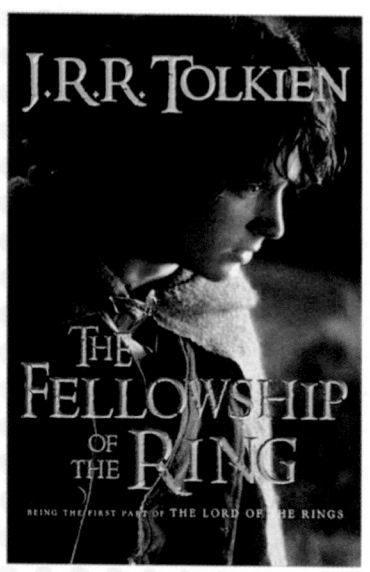

THE REVIEW: "no guy on guy action - the only thing that makes these kinds of patriarchial stories worth the read. in my version of the story, aragorn is getting it on with the pretty legolas who wears braids and a miniskirt. the dwarf has to be jealous because you know something is going on between him and the elf."

Ma'am, we have some good news for you about certain types of writing that are available on the Internet.

★☆☆☆☆

THE PRODUCT: *Anna Karenina,* by Leo Tolstoy

THE REVIEW: "Just because you CAN write a 1,000 page book, doesn't mean you SHOULD."

Could have been summed up quite easily in a four-panel comic. Like Cathy. *Why wasn't this just covered in* Cathy?

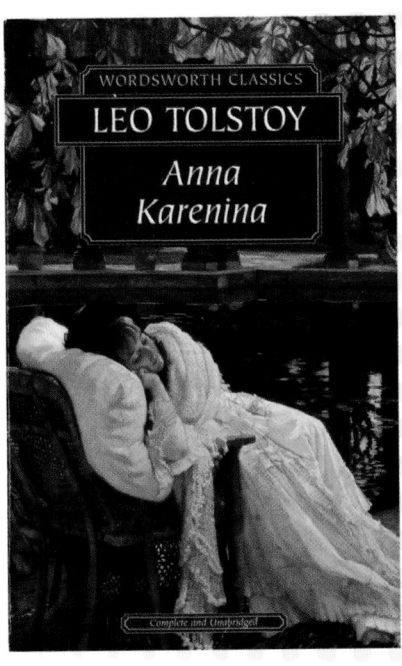

★☆☆☆☆

THE PRODUCT: *Crime and Punishment,* by Fyodor Dostoevsky

THE REVIEW: "All the characters have at least three or four unpronounceable, multi-syllabic Russian names, making them almost impossible to keep track of, even if you cared."

You should pick up the translation where all of the characters are named Tony. That bit when impoverished student Tony brutally murders Tony and is forced to kill the innocent bystander Tony as well—man, it was intense.

★☆☆☆☆

THE PRODUCT: *Jurassic Park* (1993)

THE REVIEW: ". . . spineless anti-gun nonsense, where only the 'bad guys' fend-off the big-teeth Dino's using (ohmygawsh) guns, and poor Goldblum is stuck using only a baseball bat."

I think this reviewer must have seen a different movie than everyone else, possibly one that he imagined while high. Then again, if I ever saw a movie that was just Jeff Goldblum beating the hell out of velociraptors with a baseball bat, I wouldn't be satisfied with plain Jurassic Park, *either.*

⭐⭐⭐⭐⭐

THE PRODUCT: *Game of Thrones*, HBO, 2011–Present

THE REVIEW: "They dwarf was annoyingly short for my taste. And they all acted like they were from the medieval times."

Game of Thrones would have been much better if all the characters acted like they were grunge fans from 1990s Seattle. Instead of warfare, you'd have morose, passive-aggressive angst battles with lots of indoor drinking. Instead of dragons, you'd have . . . do they have dragons in Seattle? I've never been there.

THE PRODUCT: *The Shawshank Redemption* (1994)

THE REVIEW: "It isn't even courageous enough to admit that it is a gay love story."

And The Lion King *wasn't courageous enough to admit to its "Kill and Eat All Humans and Take Over Their Cities Because We're Sentient Goddamn Lions" message. When will Hollywood grow a pair?*

★★★★★

THE PRODUCT: Harry Potter and the Half-Blood Prince Bad Group: Collector's Beaded Bookmark

THE REVIEW: "ALAN RICKMAN PLAYS A GOOD GUY IN THIS MOVIE!!!I KONW FOR SOME OF YOU YOU CANT UNDERSTAND THAT BUT HE IS!!!!!!!!!!!!"

YEAH, SNAPE WAS SOME GOOD GUY ALL RIGHT. ESPECIALLY THE WAY HE GOT REJECTED BY A GIRL IN HIGH SCHOOL AND LATER INDIRECTLY CAUSED HER DEATH AND THEN DECIDED TO ATONE FOR THAT BY EMOTIONALLY TORTURING HER SURVIVING ONLY CHILD AND—wait, wait. Can't you see that this Harry Potter Collector's Beaded Bookmark is tearing us apart?

★☆☆☆☆

THE PRODUCT: *The Hunger Games* (2012)

THE REVIEW: "I was looking forward to this movie for months and have read through the books going on 3 times . . . . The 'fire' if that's what you even want to call it, that was suppose to engulf Katniss' wardrobe was the lamest excuse for fire I have ever seen. It looked like a cheap production trick."

Why didn't they simply set Jennifer Lawrence on fire? Cheaper and more realistic.

★★★★★

THE PRODUCT: *Expendables* Action Figure: Barney Ross

THE REVIEW: "As a longtime and hardcore fan of Stallone and his films, I find this figure to be an extreme waste of potential . . . . The figure's face sculpt is nothing short of an insulting cartoon interpretation of Sly."

To be fair, "an insulting cartoon interpretation of Sly" is a pretty good description of what Sylvester Stallone's actual face looks like these days.

Chapter 6
ENTITLEMENT a-GO-GO

We hear a lot about "entitlement" these days, mostly in the form of complaints about America's millennial generation. But it turns out that entitlement is most prevalent not among our much-maligned, selfie-taking younglings, but among a subset of Internet reviewers. When the service-people of the world don't eagerly bow down to comb the dust and grime from their toe hair, these people get mad enough to leave a keyboard-shattering bad review.

★☆☆☆☆

THE PRODUCT: Subsolo Spanish Restaurant & Bar, Sydney, Australia

THE REVIEW: "If a waiter gets a little cheeky, put him/ her in his/her place. Come on people, peppy service is good and a quip always deserves a quip back, not soft-skinned limp attitude."

"Grab the waiter by the back of the neck and shake him to establish dominance. If waiter continues to pee on your furniture, work on developing eye contact and voice levels until waiter acknowledges you as pack leader."

THE PRODUCT: Hooters Restaurant, Culpeper, VA

THE REVIEW: " . . . I was not satisfied with her figure at all. I am a lonely guy and when I go out I expect to see some double d *** and a J LO ***!!!"

And until the end of time, it remained a complete mystery as to why this guy was lonely.

★☆☆☆☆

THE PRODUCT: Walt Disney World, Orlando, FL

THE REVIEW: " . . . my magical dreams were burst into sadness and disappointment when I reached your theme parks."

If you're over eighteen years old and still have "magical dreams" about Disney World, you might want to back out of any jury-duty summons you get in the near future. Unless they involve the prosecution of a lovable talking animal, in which case you're all set.

THE PRODUCT: Walt Disney World, Orlando, FL

THE REVIEW: "Denied of allowing [my son] to have a line pass, which another employee suggested i ask for one since he was having a melt down in the line. I didn't know you had to fall under certain guidelines to be given a pass."

There are no guidelines at all about who's given front-of-the-line passes at theme parks. All those people waiting in line without passes are just there because they enjoy the view of the person in front's back sweat.

THE PRODUCT: Conspiracy Tattoo, Wagga Wagga, Australia

THE REVIEW: "Worst tattooist ever, went to this place for my first tattoo. Was something very simple, he used a stencil and put it on,upside down (yes, I should have checked it)."

"I should have glanced down at the indelible mark the tattooist was about to leave on my skin, but I was really caught up in that '17 Ways to Get Your Cat to Like You' article in Cats Plus *magazine."*

★★★★★

THE PRODUCT: Sala Spa Massage, Phuket, Thailand

THE REVIEW: "took a oil massage, didn't expect a guy to do the massage for me . . . what a turn off . . . "

It's because of people like this guy that the massage parlor had to put a "NO SEX" warning on their sign. Clearly, they also needed to include a crude stick-figure diagram, and maybe put on one of those educational sock-puppet plays beforehand.

THE PRODUCT: Walmart.com

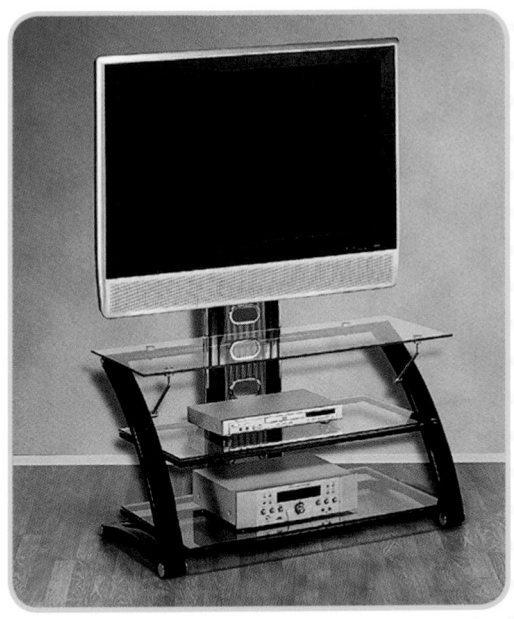

THE REVIEW: "Wal-Mart ruined Christmas for my family . . . . The only thing that [my son] asked Santa for was a television . . . . The truck never showed up . . . . My parents drove to my house on Christmas Eve and put their gifts for my son under the Christmas tree so he would have something to open . . . . Wal-Mart dropped the ball and a child did without on Christmas."

There's nothing sadder in this world than an American child wanting his own television for Christmas, and only getting a bunch of other presents instead. Well, maybe human trafficking and genocide, but not by much.

★★★★★

THE PRODUCT: SkyMall Pull-Up Christmas Tree

THE REVIEW: "When we got it many spheres were broken and half of the lights did not light up . . . . Ruined our Christmas ended up buying a real tree instead"

"And Mary brought forth her firstborn son, and wrapped him in swaddling clothes, and laid him in a manger, because there was no room for them in the inn, and lo, Mary did say: 'This fully booked inn hath ruined our Christmas.'"

THE PRODUCT: Vroman's Bookstore, Pasadena, CA

THE REVIEW: "I dont like Vromans and I have a valid reason. I only go to bookstores to read their tabloid magazines for free! I usually buy my books online since its way cheaper. Anyways, Vromans has ALL their magazines on racks outside in front of their store. First of all they don't provide tables (outside) for you to read. Secondly, the attendant outside is always glaring at you if you start flipping through a magazine for more than five minutes."

Vroman's Free Tabloid and Book Sampling Warehouse Staffed by Pixies Who Get Paid in Magical Pixie Dust did not respond for comment.

★★★★★

THE PRODUCT: Cornbread Cafe: Vegan Comfort Food, Eugene, OR

THE REVIEW: "For those who avoid soy, pasta, corn and gluten there's not much to eat here. Won't be back."

A vegan restaurant called "Cornbread Cafe" that serves grains? And corn? And bread? Next thing we'll be hearing about a skydiving company that doesn't cater to people with deathly parachute phobias and who also hate airplanes.

Chapter 7

DON'T ADD KIDS

Kids are wonderful: All you have to do is feed them, water them, and maybe spray them now and then to keep the insects off, and in only a few years, they'll grow into full-size humans! Something about the presence of these little people-larvae, however, makes a lot of online reviewers go crazy. A movie titled *Goreviolence 5000: The Punchening* made your six-year-old cry at the cinema? Store clerks weren't thrilled with your decision to let your free-spirited three-year-old run loose in their antique glassware store? There's only one thing to do: Unleash your fury online.

★☆☆☆☆

THE PRODUCT: *Good Luck Charlie,* Disney Channel

THE REVIEW: "There is no other child and family who loves 'Disney' more than us. But that all changed when you chose to air the two mommies episode of Good Luck Charlie last week . . . my son knows the 'true' Disney now. All of his Disney dreams and fantasies gone."

Wait until he turns thirteen. I assure you that every single one of those Disney fantasies involving two mommies will come roaring back.

THE PRODUCT: *Good Luck Charlie,* Disney Channel

THE REVIEW: "people were blaming the dad character for the birth of charlie and them guess WHAT HE SAID. ' hey, dont be mad at me, it takes 2 people to make a baby.' I AM SO SO SOS SO SOS OS SO JFAJKF WAT EVER MAD"

Personally, I want my son growing up believing that making a baby requires at least five people. He'll be so overwhelmed by the thought of what sex must require that he'll never even ask a girl out.

★★★★★

THE PRODUCT: Holly Shores Camping Resort, Cape May, NJ

THE REVIEW: "My daughter rang the bell, nobody came so she rang it again. This rude boss lady yelled at my daughter: 'Don't you see me talking to someone? I'll be with you when I'm done!' . . . To a 10 year old, you ring the bell until someone comes to help you."

How else is a ten-year-old meant to know that continuously ringing a bell is not appropriate? If only this wisdom could be imparted somehow, by someone close to the child . . . via some sort of communication made possible by Homo sapiens' large brains, descended larynxes, and well-developed vocal cords . . . ah well, I guess it's hopeless.

★☆☆☆☆

THE PRODUCT: The Dairy Bar & Bistro, London, United Kingdom

THE REVIEW: ". . . the cocktails we started with were great . . . . My son was getting agitated, crying etc, he does this when he is hungry, so I began to breastfeed him. The manageress came back with our brandies and just looked at me, disgusted . . . how could another woman try to make me feel ashamed about doing something natural?"

How could another person judge this woman for naturally feeding her baby with natural milk that's been naturally imbued with natural cocktails and natural brandy? Alcoholic breastmilk: it's nature's Ambien.

★☆☆☆☆

THE PRODUCT: Ingles Market, Hendersonville, NC

THE REVIEW: "my baby threw up on my husband . . . the cashier abby said u cant even clean your childs mess up i was pissed . . . . So she told me to leave honestly i wanted to grave her up and beat the living daylights out of her but i didn't . . ."

On the plus side, condom sales in Abby's store went up 87 percent that day.

★☆☆☆☆

THE PRODUCT: Sylvan Complete At-Home System: School Success, Ages 8-12

THE REVIEW: "In the story, it said that birds are related to crocodiles. That is evolution. That is a theory and should not be imposed on my child no more than religion."

It's rare to meet someone who opposes both evolution and religion being taught to children. Presumably she has now formed her own educational curriculum containing only pure mathematics and an intensive course on the correct way to cook bacon.

THE PRODUCT:
Better Bedding, Orange, CT

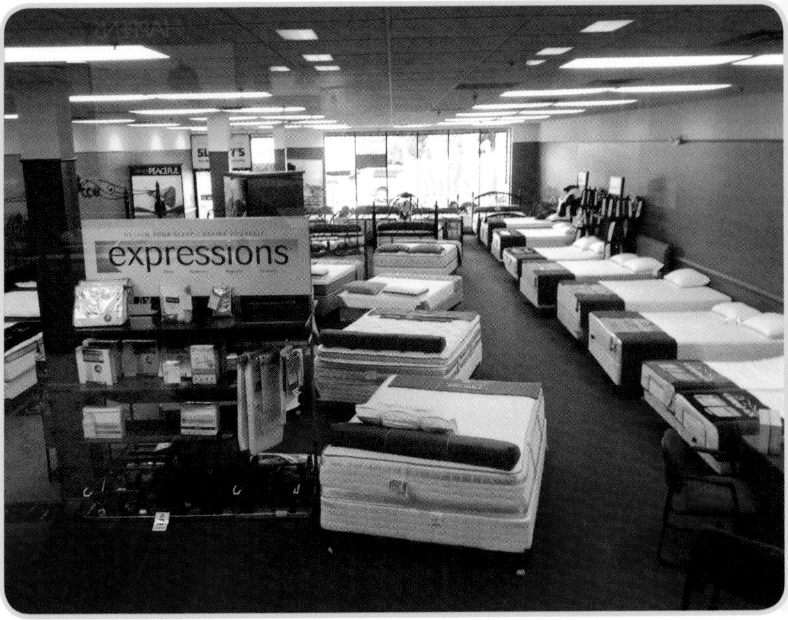

THE REVIEW: "I have just left the Orange store and should have called the cops now that I think about it . . . . My older son who is 10 and Autistic jumped up on the be3d. The mans response was son if your shoes are dirty get off the bed."

And then he could have jumped on the roof of the cop car as well.

★★★★★

THE PRODUCT: Walmart, Liberty, MO

THE REVIEW: "i spent 730 dollars and as i was leaving the manager said i was banned for life due to she said i was yelling at my kids, my son run off back in december and my kid pee'ed on the floor."

This lady's child has been living in a Walmart since December. Sleeping on the display beds. Eating in the produce section. Finding . . . himself. Lost In Walmart, starring Shia LaBeouf. Coming this summer.

THE PRODUCT: Johnson's Baby Bubble Bath & Wash

THE REVIEW: "This was the first time my 21 month old son had a bubble bath and honestly the bubbles scared my son."

She also voiced her complaints to the water utility company, to several faucet manufacturers, and to Sulis, the Roman god of baths.

★☆☆☆☆

THE PRODUCT: Ben Franklin Store, Amherst, OH

THE REVIEW: " . . . he told me that I shouldn??t bring my kids in the store. I COULD NOT believe it. He said well I should not let them pick up stuff and put it all over the store. Sure my kids were looking at stuff and they may not have put everything they touched back but they are children and I was doing my best to make sure that they were putting the stuff back."

"They only took like, 30 percent of the guy's inventory. Tops."

THE PRODUCT: My Little Pony Nightmare Moon Figure

THE REVIEW: "I was unaware it lit up and spoke in such a evil tone of voice. I would not reccomend this toy for any child under 8 or 9. This toy may give them nightmares."

If only they hadn't named the toy "Super Daydream Non-Evil Pony Figure," and then you would have had some sort of advance warning.

PART II

TERRIBLE STUFF

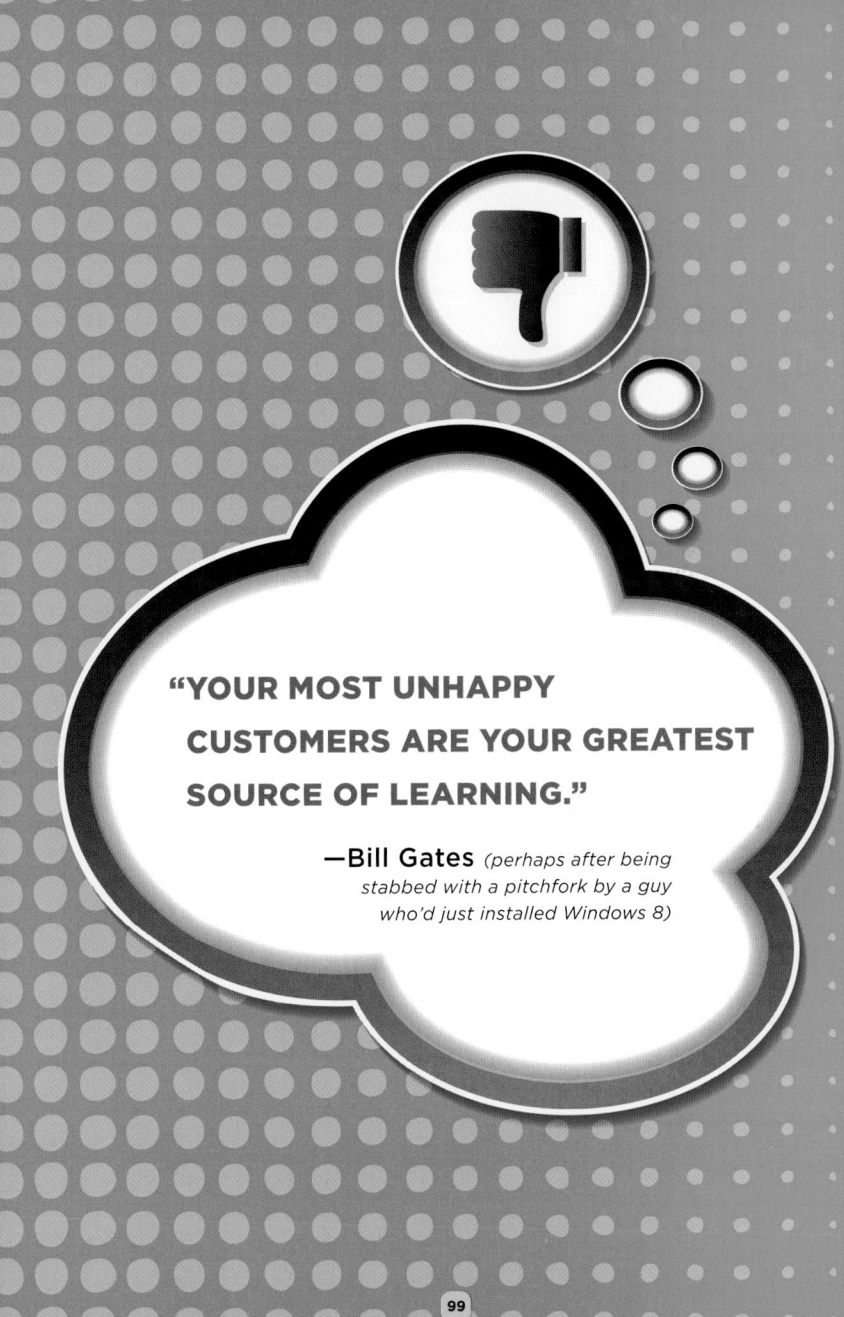

"YOUR MOST UNHAPPY
CUSTOMERS ARE YOUR GREATEST
SOURCE OF LEARNING."

—**Bill Gates** *(perhaps after being
stabbed with a pitchfork by a guy
who'd just installed Windows 8)*

Chapter 8
One-STaR PRODUCTS

Sometimes reviewers are the ones getting things wrong. But other times, the products themselves are terrible in ways that most of us could never imagine. The items in this chapter didn't just break, or ship incorrectly, or even look different than they did in the advertisement. No, these are products that defy the very borders of awfulness, like some kind of Border Patrol agent who reaches across the border just to punch small animals.

★☆☆☆☆

THE PRODUCT: Mood Finger Scan App by Indigo Penguin Limited

THE REVIEW: "Is mini touch broken or is this a bad app? It said restless, than sad (I Was happy, I JUST HAD A CHEESECAKE!!!), than it said relaxed, please fix this guys, this could be a better app!!!"

Any mood-scanning app that can't even detect cheesecake happiness should be banned. Even perfect-wedding-to-your-true-love-and-then-finding-a-winning-lottery-ticket-in-the-church-bathroom-level happiness only measures out to around 0.95 on the cheesecake scale.

★☆☆☆☆

THE PRODUCT: Hanes Big Men's Flannel Pajama Set

THE REVIEW: "After searching everywhere for pajamas for my husband to wear in our christamas photo we found these and were so excited until 10 min into our photo shoot the front of the pants completely ripped out."

Not sure what you guys were doing in that photo shoot, or if I'd personally ever want to put one of your family Christmas cards on my own mantel shelf, but sorry about the pants.

up to 5XL

★☆☆☆☆

THE PRODUCT: Diana's Care Home, Hayward, CA

THE REVIEW: "My father caught fire mysteriously at this place and I would NOT recommend that you take your loved ones to this horrible place."

And the award for completely unnecessary second clause of a sentence goes to . . . .

★☆☆☆☆

THE PRODUCT: Bondi Ink Tattoo, Bondi Beach, Australia

THE REVIEW: "I have murk on my body instead of mark."

Just tattoo "No Ragrets" under it and you'll be set.

★☆☆☆☆

THE PRODUCT: Clean Eau de Parfum

THE REVIEW: "A gross mix of lemon pledge and windex. If you wear this, people will think you have been cleaning the house. It also smells like a moderately well maintained public bathroom."

"Ramon!" cried Sarah as she sank into her lover's passionate embrace. The sweet scent of a moderately well-maintained public bathroom reached Ramon's nostrils as he clasped Sarah to his muscled chest.

★★★★★

THE PRODUCT: Tink's Miss November Doe Decoy

THE REVIEW: "I put the fake deer in the garden and deer attacked it. Now the back end won't keep air in it."

What did the deer do to the fake doe in your backyard, ma'am? Can you show us on this anatomically correct deer doll?

THE PRODUCT: *Valhalla Rising* (2009)

THE REVIEW: "The most exciting moment (here comes the spoiler)occurs towards the end when several characters walk up a hill. I kid you not, that's all that happens, they walk up a hill, but compared to the sheer inertia of the preceding events, the moment is quite exciting."

Yeah, but did they get to the top of the hill? *Don't leave us hanging!*

★☆☆☆☆

THE PRODUCT: Techko S096 Solar Powered Vibration Sensor Entry Alarm

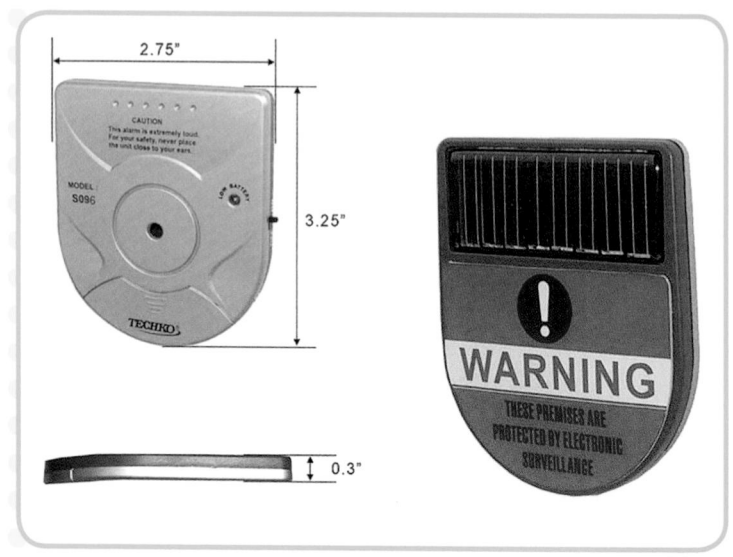

THE REVIEW: "On the first day I mounted it on my window with little morning sun shinning on the window caused the batteries, located in the back to explode. The batteries went airborne to another room like bullets."

Later, it became the first solar-powered entry alarm to star in its own action movie.

THE PRODUCT: SQUEELER R/C
All Terrain Vehicle

THE REVIEW: "Caught fire after about 20 mins of use. Returned after it caught fire, my grandson was really disappointed."

Disappointed? Most grandsons are delighted when fire appears in a place where formerly there was no fire. I'm surprised you didn't order more.

★★★★★

THE PRODUCT: Thierry Mugler Womanity Eau de Parfum

THE REVIEW: "This smells like old margarine first, then it smells like margarine mixed with rancid grapefruit, then it smells like all that with pine sol mixed in. Then as it wafts into the air the vapors smell like garbage."

Another reviewer described it as "the smell of decomposing flesh and some rotten mangos," so at least this scent is stimulating everyone's imaginations.

THE PRODUCT: Yatagan Eau de Toilette by Caron

THE REVIEW: " . . . smelled like the inside of particle-board kitchen cupboard in a mobile home."

"Drove girls wild. I bought twelve bottles."

★✩✩✩✩

THE PRODUCT: Just Kidz 18 in. Good Kids Doll

THE REVIEW: "Once my daughter got it, she was terrified of the back of the dolls head. It had no hair!! Her hair was pulled in pigtails and was completely empty on the back."

The best thing to do would have been to draw another face on the back of the doll's head, explain to your daughter that real people have an evil face hiding under their hair just like the doll, and then tell her that she should watch out for people walking backward into her bedroom at night.

ONLY AT
K
kmart

THE PRODUCT: Miss BIC for Her Medium Ballpoint Pen (Box of 12), Black

THE REVIEW: "Where are the 'For Him' pens? . . . Am I destined to just watch all of the women around me falling into a sparkly dream of ponies, crochet and butterflies, while I pace angrily here, unable to access the manly world of construction vehicles, barbeques, motor racing and science?"

Real men write any necessary messages in smearings of their own manly blood, or just yell really loudly at passing animals.

THE PRODUCT: Smart Border Collie Sticker

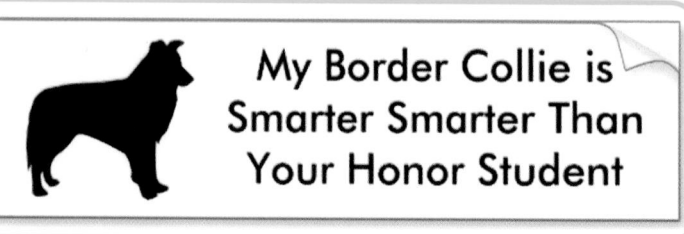

My Border Collie is Smarter Smarter Than Your Honor Student

THE REVIEW: "Grammatical error! Make sure this is edited before your purchase. Notice: 'smarter' doubled."

Honestly, you should just be impressed that a border collie can even write and design a sticker at all. How did he even hold the stylus?

THE PRODUCT: Veet Fast Acting Gel Cream Hair Remover For Legs & Body

THE REVIEW: "I used this prior to a trip so I would not have to shave. Unfortunately, it didn't remove the hair but did remove my skin."

The reviewer selected "pleasant scent" as a "pro" of this product, so she can obviously teach us something about looking on the bright side.

Chapter 9
one-STAR Restaurants

We've all had less-than-enviable dining experiences. The service is slow; the drinks are overpriced; the waiter looks down on you when you ask for peanut butter on your steak. But none of this compares to the *exceptionally* bad restaurant experience. Scattered around the Internet are tales of waiters who insult us to our faces, of human body parts in food, and other things that will make you want to stay home in your sweatpants and just eat a microwave dinner. You won't even mind the frozen bit in the middle.

★☆☆☆☆

THE PRODUCT: Colony Cafe, Miami Beach, FL

THE REVIEW: "My girl Lisa orders a Margarita (beverage), downs it, asks for her 2nd 'free' one and then asks how much tequila is in it. The server asks back, 'There's tequila in a margarita?'"

Next they'll be telling the server that he wasn't supposed to put pizza sauce and cheese in there.

★☆☆☆☆

THE PRODUCT: Amelia's Restaurant, Dutch Harbor, AK

THE REVIEW: " . . . i found a tooth in my food, i told the waitress, and she didn't believe me. I paid for the whole meal regardless, couple minutes later i ended up vomiting my food, then 30 minutes I vomited again."

You know what's worse than finding a tooth in your food? Finding a tooth in your food and then noticing that the meatloaf was half-price that day, and that one of the waiters is mysteriously missing.

★☆☆☆☆

THE PRODUCT: Compadre's, Englewood, FL

THE REVIEW: " . . . I found a hair in my taco, and then the waiter accused me of planting it there . . . . I'm 62 and gray, and the hair was black."

Come on, guys. No one saves up their last non-gray hair and then wastes it in a taco. You put it under your pillow for the Age Fairy, and in return she brings you an AARP membership card and a Rolling Stones reunion ticket.

THE PRODUCT: Bucatini Restaurant & Bar, Mitcham, Australia

THE REVIEW: "I found glass in my food, and when the manager was informed he very rudely accused me of putting there."

"I was so surprised that my monocle fell out and landed in my dish, which only made things worse."

★☆☆☆☆

THE PRODUCT: Chinaman's Hat Restaurant, Sorrento, Australia

THE REVIEW: " . . . when we poured our tea there were bits of food in it (at least that's what we hoped it was!)."

Those hopes were dashed when the pieces started moving and formed a crude "WASH ME" message on the surface of the tea.

★☆☆☆☆

THE PRODUCT: Anthony's Pasta Bar, Syracuse, NY

THE REVIEW: "The waiter was very slow and when we asked for more bread he misheard us and came over with ANOTHER bottle of wine. When we explained to him we are sorry but actually asked for bread not wine he replied with 'well aren't you guys geniuses'."

"Sure, fire me, Mr. Smith, but where are you going to find another person who can carry a bottle of wine all the way from the bar to the table in under ten minutes? That's right, NOWHERE."

THE PRODUCT: Blundell Arms, Horwich, United Kingdom

![The Blundell Arms]

THE REVIEW: "The waiter actually dropped one plate and put the food back onto to it and placed it on the table expecting us to eat it. The food splattered all over the floor, a chair and my own trousers."

At least he didn't yell "five-second rule!" while doing it.

★☆☆☆☆

THE PRODUCT: Hungry Jack's, Joondalup, Australia

THE REVIEW: " . . . birds are feeding off tables, rubbish & spilled drinks on floor . . . ."

The restaurant owners brought in those birds to try to solve the restaurant's insect problem. Then they tried to bring in a bunch of bird-eating spiders to solve the bird problem, but that just didn't go well at all.

★☆☆☆☆

THE PRODUCT: Sushi Tango, Minneapolis, MN

THE REVIEW: "My date had lipstick on his glass and didn't notice until he had drank almost his half his beer. When we notified the waitress she didn't seem concerned about this and instead asked 'why he was wearing lipstick.'"

And that was just ridiculous, because he was wearing coral peach, whereas the glass was smeared with more of a plum color.

⭐☆☆☆☆

THE PRODUCT: Soprano Cafe & Italian Restaurant, Miami Beach, FL

THE REVIEW: "At the end of the night, we were surrounded, threatened, and told that we could not leave until we had ordered more drinks."

"Your menfolk must order colorful, girly drinks with those little umbrellas in them. We will then take pictures and post them online with hilariously demeaning captions."

★☆☆☆☆

THE PRODUCT: Old Chicago Pizza & Taproom, Madison, WI

THE REVIEW: " . . . the waiter spilled cocktail sauce on my wife, then started laughing. She went to the bathroom to clean up and was so overwhelmed by the stench that she had to leave immediately. On our way out they ran after us, thinking that we were leaving without paying our bill. In order to get to our car we had to cross a huge, busy street to get to the mall parking lot and nearly got run over by a cab."

But apart from that, how was the meal?

★☆☆☆☆

THE PRODUCT: Alf's Ice Cream and Burgers, McMinnville, OR

THE REVIEW: " . . . the monkeys are creepy. They watch you from inside their cage while you eat your food. Eventually we moved to the patio area, so we didn't have to look at them."

Nothing improves one's burger-eating experience like the forlorn gaze of a few sad, caged intelligent creatures . . . especially if the number of monkeys keeps going down every time you visit.

★☆☆☆☆

THE PRODUCT: Maine-Ly New England, Zephyrhills, FL

THE REVIEW: "The waitress sneezed at least 5 times into her hands while taking our order. When asked if she was planning to wash her hands she made a funny gesture with her face."

Silly restaurant patrons. Don't they know that the mercury in hand-washing soap has been scientifically linked to autism?

★☆☆☆☆

THE PRODUCT: Chez Sovan, Campbell, CA

THE REVIEW: "The lasttime we were there I ordered some kind of red meat dish, thinkingthat it was beef (as it said on the menu) although it tasted nothing like any beef I'de ever had. It had a very strange, nauseating smellthat was reminiscent of what dog might taste like."

The Canine Anti-Defamation Society objects to your smear of dog meat as "strange" and "nauseating," and also requests that you scratch them right there. Aw yeah, that's the spot.

★☆★★★

THE PRODUCT: Sinbad's Pier 2 Restaurant, San Francisco, CA

THE REVIEW: "As I walked in on a dare unto myself, Sinbad himself greeted us as we entered. No, not the comedian, but the Arabian Nights Sailor. It was a life size wax statue. With chest hair seemingly made of pubes. Who's hungry?"

It took them weeks to bribe enough homeless people to collect those chest-hair pubes, and all you can do is criticize.

★☆★★★

THE PRODUCT: Madeira Cafe, Cape Town, South Africa

THE REVIEW: "When we got home we discovered that we only got the starter and one main, instead of two mains which we paid for. We called the restaurant and the waiter accused us of leaving without paying . . . . He then said he's putting the manager on the phone, the manager grabbed the phone and screamed at me 'Fuck You!!!'"

Later the manager went to the reviewer's house and threw the missing entrée, tied to a brick, through his window.

THE PRODUCT: Casa Bonita, Lakewood, CO

THE REVIEW: "My girlfriend was in a wheelchair . . . . The staff completely ignored her, even when she spoke directly to them. I told them not to ask me if she wants a soda, ask her. Blank stares all around, and they continued to pretend she didn't exist."

"Sorry sir, we don't speak wheelchair. This is America."

THE PRODUCT: International House of Pancakes, Detroit, MI

THE REVIEW: "The waitress came up with menus and announced in a very loud voice that she would be back to take our orders after she goes to the bathroom because and I quote 'I can't hold this (I will omit what she said she was holding) in any longer.'"

It was a song, right? She couldn't hold in the song that was inside her?

Chapter 10

ONE-STAR HOTELS

The world is full of hotel-review sites to help wise travelers choose their temporary sleep-holes. And if those sites are to be believed, the world is also full of terrible hotels. Check carefully before you expose your soft, defenseless, unconscious human body to eight hours in a hotel establishment's care. Or else you might end up staying at a place like . . . .

THE PRODUCT: Club Aqua Gumbet Hotel, Gumbet, Turkey

THE REVIEW: "The TVs and beds were being repossessed as we were there . . . There was no cleaners as they had already walked out for not being paid for 6 weeks, no towels let alone clean ones. The pool was green, and was nothing like any pictures that were taken.

I hope they didn't also repossess the boss's "Hotel Owner of the Year" plaque.

★☆☆☆☆

THE PRODUCT: Travelodge Wembley, London, United Kingdom

THE REVIEW: "Most of the night we could notice a horrible smell through the night but we didn't know where it was from. When we got up my friend opend the bible for some reason and we noticed someone had taking a poo in the bible!"

"Mr. Dawkins? Your friends and family are here because we're starting to think you might have a problem."

★☆☆☆☆

THE PRODUCT: Holiday Inn Hotel & Suites Boston-Peabody, Peabody, MA

THE REVIEW: "I was staying in room 109 that night and the meth lab and explosion occurred just before midnight . . . ."

When your description of a hotel stay doubles as a good opening line for a hardboiled crime novel, you're probably entitled to write a bad review.

THE PRODUCT: Hotel Erwin, Venice Beach, CA

THE REVIEW: "When my turn [in line] finally came, a burly guy swooped in and served a visibly shaken front desk clerk with a subpoena to appear in court."

"Sir, you must appear in court for the crime of . . . running an awesome hotel! *Wait, why are all your guests leaving?"*

★☆☆☆☆

THE PRODUCT: Hotel Fellini, Rome, Italy

THE REVIEW: "I particularly enjoyed the really loud sex noise coming from the English couple staying next to my room . . . ."

I'm just impressed that the normally-so-reserved English are capable of having noisy sex. How does that even work? Do they just shout "JOLLY GOOD! JOLLY GOOD!" over and over again?

★☆☆☆☆

THE PRODUCT: Belgrove Hotel, London, United Kingdom

THE REVIEW: "Brilliantly, the toilet wasn't actually fixed to the floor, like some kind of cunning booby-trap for the weary contortionist defecator."

How else are you supposed to empty the toilet into the sink when it gets full? You tell me, genius.

THE PRODUCT: Grand Paradise Playa Dorada, Puerto Plata, Dominican Republic

THE REVIEW: " . . . the special of the night was taco's but they were out of taco shells. We made reservations for there special Italian restaurant and had pizza the base was taco shells."

Did you at least go back and tell them you'd solved the mystery of the missing taco shells?

THE PRODUCT: Grand Paradise Playa Dorada, Puerto Plata, Dominican Republic

THE REVIEW: "Some of the male guests had prostitutes as their guests. One prostitue had her teen daughter and toddler son with her. The didn't have any programs for teens . . . ."

Well, where else was the prostitute's teen daughter supposed to go? The hotel didn't have any teen programs for her!

★☆☆☆☆

THE PRODUCT: Knights Inn Nashville-Antioch, Antioch, TN

THE REVIEW: "There was a very unpleasant note written on the one 'do not disturb' door signs – so we threw it away. (having gay sex)"

Everyone knows that if you're really serious about keeping maids out, you just draw a quick outline of a bunny suit.

★☆☆☆☆

THE PRODUCT: Town Inn Suites, Toronto, Canada

THE REVIEW: "One of the rooms had a hole in the floor in the bathroom and you could see the into the room underneath."

"On the plus side, my downstairs neighbor gave me a great recommendation for an effective athlete's-foot cream."

THE PRODUCT: Cabins For You, Gatlinburg, TN

THE REVIEW: "There were cobwebs everywhere and there was a web on the chandelier over the kitchen table with hundreds of baby spiders crawling on it."

I sincerely hope you set fire to the place. And then salted the earth that surrounds it.

THE PRODUCT: Tulsa Select Hotel and Conference Center, Tulsa, OK

THE REVIEW: "Police raided the hotel and busted two meth labs. They came to our door, rushed us out of the hotel becuae we were in danger. Hotel refused to give us our money back . . . ."

Yeah, but could you actually prove *that there were more meth labs in that hotel than you would find in the average suburban living room? I mean, who* hasn't *found a clandestine volatile organic chemical manufacturing site or two behind a sofa cushion?*

★☆☆☆☆

THE PRODUCT: Hilton Head Metropolitan Hotel, Hilton Head Island, SC

THE REVIEW: "When I went to the front desk to ask about the air conditioning the same disgruntled employee pulled out a junky fan and said 'here's the a.c..'"

At least you didn't ask him about the shower.

★☆☆☆☆

THE PRODUCT: Knights Inn South Bend, South Bend, IN

THE REVIEW: "We stayed in a room where the bathroom floor was LITERALLY FALLING IN. The toilet was FALLING THROUGH THE FLOOR."

Knights Inn simply wanted to re-create the realistic level of sanitation that an actual medieval knight would have experienced. Stop being so close-minded and grab yourself some hay and wet leaves to wipe with.

THE PRODUCT: Travelodge Palm Springs, Palm Springs, CA

THE REVIEW: "On my birthday, I was woken up by the loud owners kicking out a homeless man that made it into the pool area. The owner spent 30 minutes calling him every foul name in the book and threatened to beat him up."

"It was the best birthday ever."

★☆☆☆☆

THE PRODUCT: Akai Motel, Alberta, Canada

THE REVIEW: " . . . we turned off the lights and got into bed just after a few minutes when it was dark you started to hear things move in the walls on the floor everywhere . . . . Then my wife looked at me and said that she thinks she felt something by her foot, so then she jumped out of bed and I pulled the sheets back and seen a huge cockroach or some kind of beetle but after smashing it with my boot and trying to kill it it just would not die."

They're Canadian bugs. The trick is to ask them politely to leave and maybe offer them a lift to the nearest Tim Hortons.

★☆☆☆☆

THE PRODUCT: Howard Johnson Inn and Suites, Ashland, VA

THE REVIEW: "It could use a little updating and new carpets. There was also this creepy mirror that took up the whole wall behind the beds almost as if someone was watching you."

"Occasional coughing sound from behind the mirror did not ease my mind."

THE PRODUCT: Artisan Hotel Boutique, Las Vegas, NV

THE REVIEW: "Very dark hallways with red lighting and disturbing paintings literally covering every inch of the walls and ceilings . . . . We had to cover up one of the paintings in our room just so I could sleep . . . ."

"At 3 a.m., I woke up to find that the covering had fallen off and the eyes of the person in the painting were pointed in my direction. The voice of the demon Pazuzu asked me if I needed any more towels."

Chapter 11
ONE-STAR BOOKS

The writer of the self-published fantasy epic you're reading has not seen an editor since he turned in his last high school book report. The elderly author starts a twenty-page racist rant halfway through Chapter 9. Or maybe the book's copyeditor was just drunk on the Friday night she rushed through the manuscript. If you've had this reading experience, you're not alone. The reviewers in this chapter explored the darkest caverns of the publishing world, and returned with some spine-chilling tales. (Get it? Spine? Like on a book? Yeah, I'll stop now.)

THE PRODUCT: *Secret Sins*, by Lora Leigh

THE REVIEW: "One character's name changes from Gregori to Anatoli, then back to Gregori; at one point, Cami has a conversation with herself, because of naming errors; there is a completely copied scene (and I mean it's identical) that shows up twice in the book . . . ."

When a rich, fancy, college-educated writer does it, it's called "postmodernism." When this author does it, it's called "Wait, why did you copy and paste this sex scene? Why are they doing this twice? Is there amnesia involved? Oh my god, is this hell?"

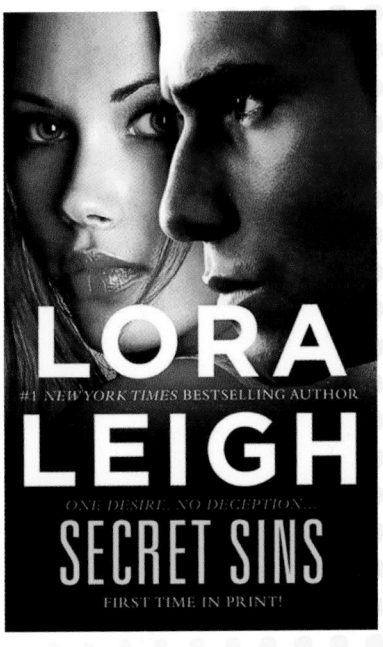

⭐⭐⭐⭐⭐

THE PRODUCT: *Breaking Dawn*
by Stephenie Meyer

breaking dawn

S T E P H E N I E   M E Y E R
AUTHOR OF THE #1 BESTSELLING *TWILIGHT, NEW MOON,* AND *ECLIPSE*

THE REVIEW: " . . . Bella, dieing and screaming in agony, vomits blood while the mutant baby inside of her destroys her body, internal organs and spine. Edward uses his teeth to bite the baby out of her uterus. . . . I was ready to drive to Arizona, find Stephenie Meyer's house, and burn it down."

I'm as tired of the old, clichéd "bite the baby out of the heroine's uterus" plot as the next person, but at least teen-pregnancy rates are probably down.

THE PRODUCT: *The Blonde Geisha,* by Jina Bacarr

THE REVIEW: "The metaphors are ridiculous . . . . I mean, come on, moon grotto? . . . Most honorable penis?"

The most harrowing scene is when the hero's penis behaves dishonorably, and he is forced to perform penis seppuku.

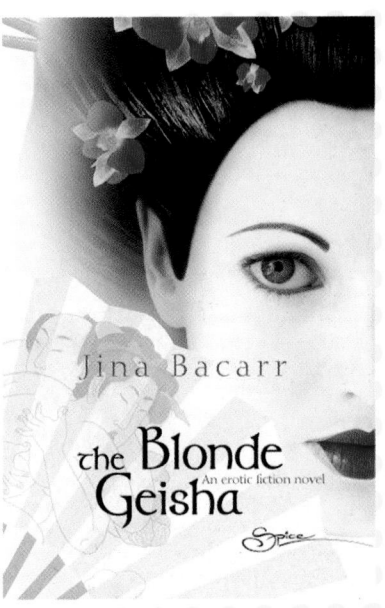

Jina Bacarr

the Blonde Geisha

An erotic fiction novel

⭐☆☆☆☆

THE PRODUCT: *Naked Sushi,* by Jina Bacarr

COSMO RED-HOT READS FROM HARLEQUIN

NAKED SUSHI
JINA BACARR

THE REVIEW: "There were moments like these: 'Coaxing my pubic hairs to flutter like daisy petals bowing to an insistent breeze.'"

Like daisy petals, the heroine's pubes are thick, bright white, and often attract swarms of bees.

THE PRODUCT: *Eternal Pleasure,* by Nina Bangs

THE REVIEW: " . . . there's a point where the dinosaurs are showing some vampires a PowerPoint presentation."

Slide 1: Escalating Company Demand for Reaching Sticks to Help with Stubby Little Dinosaur Arms.

★★★★★

THE PRODUCT: *Zombie Rain*, by Zach Sweets

THE REVIEW: "I guess I was hoping for Cormac McCarthy's *The Road* but with zombies and gay sex, but what I got instead was more *Syfy channel* cheesy than *Pulitzer prize*."

The publishing world is still waiting for The Road *except with zombies and gay sex. Believe me, I know.*

THE PRODUCT: *Pleasuring the Pirate*, by Emily Bryan

THE REVIEW: " . . . THE MAIN DUDE'S NOT ACTUALLY A PIRATE."

How can we even know who to trust anymore?

★☆☆☆☆

THE PRODUCT: *Moon People,*
by Dale M. Courtney

THE REVIEW: "I would like to nominate for execution all self publishers that allow complete piles of putrescence, like this, to be printed and released upon the unsuspecting public. I don't want punishment for these people I want professional concentrated torture."

But if Moon People *was banned, the reading public would be deprived of the* chef d'oeuvre *that* Publishers Weekly *called "the worst book ever," one that contains such epoch-defining sentences as "Suddenly everybody went right ahead and ate their breakfast" and "David looked at Cheral with a serious look on his face and leaned into Cheral and Cheral leaned in and they kissed intimently." And then where would humanity be? That's right, worse than dead.*

★★★★★

THE PRODUCT: *Midnight Sins,* by Lora Leigh

THE REVIEW: " . . . there was at least one instance where a very significant fact was revealed to the heroine and then 100 or so pages later it was revealed again by the same person, but written as if it was the first time."

Maybe the universe the book is set in was grittily rebooted within those 100 pages, like they keep doing with Spider-Man *movies.*

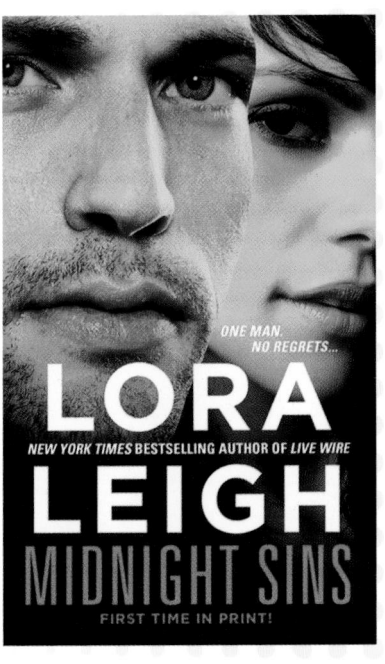

ONE MAN.
NO REGRETS...

LORA
NEW YORK TIMES BESTSELLING AUTHOR OF *LIVE WIRE*
LEIGH
MIDNIGHT SINS
FIRST TIME IN PRINT!

★☆☆☆☆

THE PRODUCT: *A Taint in the Blood*, by S.M. Stirling

THE REVIEW: "Hmmmmmmm . . . it's *really* hard to know what to say about A Taint in the Blood."

You are writing a severe, negative review of a novel called A Taint in the Blood *and you don't know what to say, reviewer?* No jokes are coming to mind?

THE PRODUCT: *The 2009-2014 World Outlook for 60-Milligram Containers of Fromage Frais*, by Professor Philip M. Parker, PhD

THE REVIEW: "A 60 milligram container would be 1/16 of a gram, or about 1/450 of an ounce. I can tell you exactly what the market outlook is for 60mg containers of fromage frais - none. There is no market outlook for 60mg containers of fromage frais, for the simple reason that they do not exist."

You're overlooking the gourmand-pixie market. There's nothing those little guys like more than a tiny cup of fromage frais topped with berries, flower nectar, and the souls of some unbaptized infants.

The 2009-2014 World Outlook for 60-Milligram Containers of Fromage Frais

by
Professor Philip M. Parker, Ph.D.
Chaired Professor of Management Science
INSEAD (Singapore and Fontainebleau, France)

★★★★★

THE PRODUCT: *Hitler: Neither Vegetarian Nor Animal Lover*, by Rynn Berry

THE REVIEW: "The author never met Hitler, nor did he find any proof that those who knew Hitler lied about his being a vegitarian animal lover."

"Joe, I know you keep telling me you're not cheating on me, but I just can't trust anything you say. I mean, you never even met Hitler."

THE PRODUCT: *The Salaryman's Wife*, by Sujata Massey

THE REVIEW: "A character invites another person to join her (but does not say where she plans on going), and the second person makes the non sequitur, 'But I shouldn't eat cake.' The first character never mentioned anything about cake."

I was going to write a comment on this review, but I shouldn't ride any more circus bears this winter.

★☆☆☆☆

THE PRODUCT: *The Big Book of Lesbian Horse Stories*, by Alisa Surkis and Monica Nolan

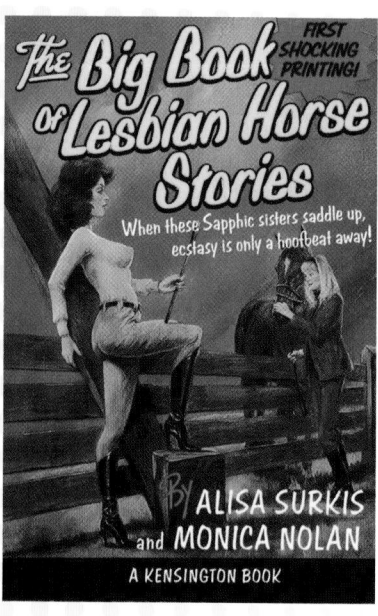

THE REVIEW: " . . . it is no larger than a regular sized book of lesbian horse stories."

I'll bet it didn't even take up a quarter of one shelf in the Lesbian Horse Stories section of Barnes and Noble.

★☆☆☆☆

THE PRODUCT: *Bombproof Your Horse: Teach Your Horse to Be Confident, Obedient, and Safe, No Matter What You Encounter*, by Rick Pelicano

THE REVIEW: "I was initially excited because I figured we could just run bombproof horses in front of our Humvee . . . . We were just hoping to get multiple uses out of each horse and that's where the book let us down. Going forward, we'll still use the horses, but we'll just stop naming them."

R.I.P. Sir Neighsalot, 2009–2009

Chapter 12
THE UNSORTED

These are the reviews that don't fit anywhere else in this book. In fact, they don't fit anywhere, period. Whether they're humorous reviews of items that are for sale for no reason known to mankind, or opinions of things that really don't need to be reviewed, this chapter welcomes them all with open, nonjudgmental arms.

THE PRODUCT: Uranium Ore

THE REVIEW: "I purchased this product 4.47 Billion Years ago and when I opened it today, it was half empty."

This is why you shouldn't put off your radioactive craft projects.

★☆☆☆☆

THE PRODUCT: Samsung UN85S9 85-Inch 4K Ultra HD 120Hz 3D Smart LED Television

THE REVIEW: "Asolutely worthless for watching midget porn. They all look normal size."

Mock the existence of an 85-inch-wide television all you like, but it totally hides the 84-inch-wide hole in my living room wall where that herd of buffalo got in.

★☆☆☆☆

THE PRODUCT: Yodok Concentration Camp, Yodok County, South Hamgyong Province, North Korea

THE REVIEW: "I can not give this gulag a 'recommend' until they invest some time and money into updating it to at LEAST Syrian or Sudanese standards."

It's like everyone lost their pride after the Berlin Wall fell. It used to be about the communism, man.

★★★★★

THE PRODUCT: Area 51, Nevada

THE REVIEW: "I couldn't find an entrance to this restraunt"

"Waiters were dressed in weird camo uniforms instead of black and white; kept shooting at me."

THE PRODUCT: Osama bin Laden's Compound, Abbottabad, Pakistan

THE REVIEW: "All sorts of people running up and down the halls at night, making all sorts of racket. Plus, I think there must be an airport really close by. I would have sworn that helicopters were landing right in the yard."

And yet strangely, this man had a better experience than many of the people in the Hotels section (Chapter 10) of this book.

THE PRODUCT: President Barack Obama (2009–present)

THE REVIEW: "Barack Hussein Obama is not half black. He is the first Arab-American President, not the first black President. Barack Hussein Obama is 50% Caucasian from his mother's side and 43.75% Arabic and 6.25% African Negro from his father's side."

Whew! I'm sure the Americans who don't like Obama for being black will be fine with a president who's almost half Arab. Now the nation can finally come together and focus on the real menace: people who walk really, really slowly in the middle of sidewalks.

★★★★★

THE PRODUCT: Mount Everest, Nepal

THE REVIEW: "The queue was ridiculous, stood there for hours next to a frozen guy who looks like he was doing the same thing. The walk-through cemetery/sanitation storage was a nice touch though. . . . Won't be going back anytime soon."

Most of the Mount Everest reviews might be jokes, but at least this guy is getting the word out that today's Everest really is a giant poop-and-corpses free-for-all. Seriously, just lock yourself in a walk-in freezer and try to hold your breath for a few hours instead; you'll have more fun.

THE PRODUCT: The United States Army

THE REVIEW: "It's a fact that vaccines contain some of the most harmful crap known to man. And you will have A LOT of vaccines during your time in the US military."

This holiday season, please spare a thought for all of our troops in harm's way . . . because of vaccines. In harm's way because of vaccines.

★☆☆☆☆

THE PRODUCT: Folsom State Prison, Represa, CA

THE REVIEW: "No trains to be seen. Johnny Cash was full of sh*t, man."

"I shot a man in Reno for this?"

★☆☆☆☆

THE PRODUCT: Leonardo DiCaprio

THE REVIEW: "Leonardo DiCaprio is a ripoff actor! His salary is bankrupting our country to live is greedy rich life style. Have you ever gone to the movies and said these tickets are too expensive? or question why you have to pay more for products that endorce films with Leonardo DiCaprio?"

James Bond stealths his way into the rich, economy-destroying villain's lair, and then gasps in horror as the man turns to face him. "So, Mr. Bond," the villain says. "I bet you're wondering why I'm Leonardo DiCaprio."

THE PRODUCT: Eiber Elementary School, Lakewood, CO

THE REVIEW: "This school is so poor! the only field trips we went on were the ones that were free and that planetarium stinks."

This is what happens when you take a nation's money out of education and put it into Leonardo DiCaprio.

⭐☆☆☆☆

THE PRODUCT: Gerbils

THE REVIEW: "i bought 2gerbils and within a week, one had killed, and strated eating the other . . . ."

Hey, at least your children learned a valuable lesson about life in our modern, capitalistic society. Try reaffirming the lesson by getting a tiny little Trump toupee for the conquering gerbil. Or maybe a Leonardo DiCaprio mask.

★☆☆☆☆

THE PRODUCT: Fascism

THE REVIEW: "What is democratic about one guy stamping his boot heel across the throat of a nation, choking the life out of it with oppressive ideology backed up by the armies and police of the state? Good riddance to this flawed setup, wherever it gets tossed out."

We look forward to this guy's shockingly iconoclastic reviews of "Throat Cancer," "Mosquitoes in Your Bedroom at Night," and "People Who Text in Movie Theaters."

★☆☆☆☆

THE PRODUCT: The 1990s

THE REVIEW: " . . . depressing grunge from that rainy city up north, crybaby socialistic Limey crap called music, and everyone thinking they were gonna solve the problems of the world by acting self-righteous and wearing Doc Martens."

The good news is that on an evolutionary timescale, the era of fashionable Dr. Martens is merely the tiniest flash of—oh no, wait. I just checked and they're about to come back in style for 40,000 years. Sorry.

★☆☆☆☆

THE PRODUCT: The English Language

THE REVIEW: "the most complicated language on earth. although this is my native tongue i'm currently learning german so one day i can quit this language altogether."

If you're reading this, thank a teacher. If you're reading this in English, thank a—well, just don't thank this guy.

THE PRODUCT: Astronauts

THE REVIEW: "i dont want to die in space"

Donate now to help end human space trafficking. It can be fatal. Full of awesome space pirates and stuff, but fatal.

acknowledge-ments

Thanks to Karen Bowe, Ingrid Dieckmann, Kimberly Cochran, A. Cartuni, E. Reid Ross, Amelia Margetts, Angie Panic, Kim Kowalski, and all the others who helped collect reviews for this book. Thanks also to Adam, for distracting the cat.

ABOUT THE AUTHOR

Born in Fiji but raised in Australia, C. Coville left her home in the Southern Hemisphere to marry into the United States Navy in 2009. She soon adapted to the sound of constant gunfire and the sensation of walking right side up, and is now a columnist and regular contributor at Cracked.com, where her writing has accumulated many millions and millions of hits. These days you can usually find her digging out of the snow in Syracuse, New York, or at *www.cscoville.com* if that's your thing.

PHOTO CREDITS

Chapter 1: You're Doing It Wrong

Last Supper Poster Print by Ron Jenkins

www.wallsthatinspire.com/religion-spiritual-religious-spirituality-posters-poster-art/Last-Supper

Niagara Parks Butterfly Conservatory, Niagara Falls, Canada

www.niagaraparks.com/niagara-falls-attractions/butterfly-conservatory.html

***Mermaids: The Body Found*, Animal Planet, 2012**

www.indiamatic.com/threads/mermaids-the-body-found-premiers-on-animal-planet.3028/

Easy Chocolate Mousse, Three Ways Recipe

www.precisionnutrition.com/cool-whip-and-i

Tender Greens Restaurant, West Hollywood, CA

www.localresearch.com/listings/tender-greens-3/

AntWorks Illuminated Combo Ant Farm

www.fatbraintoys.com/toy_companies/fascinations/antworks_illuminated_combo.cfm

***Crafting with Cat Hair: Cute Handicrafts to Make with Your Cat*, by Kaori Tsutaya**

www.amazon.com/Crafting-Cat-Hair-Cute-Handicrafts/dp/1594745250

Holy Bible: Precious Moments, Pink

www.walmart.com/ip/Precious-Moments-Bible-NKJV/10976301

Cuisinart SmartStick Extendable Shaft Hand Blender

www.cuisinart.com/discontinued/hand_blenders/csb-55n.html

Blueberry Muffins Recipe

http://commons.wikimedia.org/wiki/File:Muffin_NIH.jpg
Photo courtesy of 17Drew

Chapter 2: What Did You Expect?

HDE Prankster Shock Gag Grenade

www.amazon.com/HDE-Prankster-Grenade-Military-Enthusiasts/dp/B00884KX8E

The Violet Hour Lounge, Chicago, IL

http://gochicago.about.com/od/barsandtaverns/tp/Chicagos-mad-About-Mixology.htm
Photo courtesy of The Violet Hour Lounge

"As Seen On TV" Perfect Bacon Bowl

www.boscovs.com/shop/Product.bos?itemNumber=246448

Fatima's Psychic Studio, Salem, MA

http://tripadvisaargh.tumblr.com/ post/60254217075/she-told-me-i-was-pregnant-then-she-changed-her
Photo courtesy of taydube

LookRichForLess.com

www.ebay.com/itm/MENS-BVLGARI-Bulgari-DIAGONO-ALUMINIUM-AUTOMATIC-WATCH-AL38TA-/301080849684
Photo courtesy of collectorsbuysell

Hasbro Ouija Board Game

http://commons.wikimedia.org/wiki/ File:English_ouija_board.jpg
Photo courtesy of Mijail0711

Design Toscano Good Dog Gone Bad Peeing Bulldog Figurine

www.amazon.com/Design-Toscano-Peeing-Bulldog-QL6324/dp/ B004AB3ALG

Organism Pen Holder Sexy Ass Bum Butt Girl Toy Novelty Funny Gift Joke Present

www.amazon.com/Organism-Holder-Novelty-Funny-Present/dp/B008EK2QB4

If You Want Closure in Your Relationship Start with Your Legs: A Woman's Guide to Understanding Men, by Big Boom

www.amazon.com/Want-Closure-Your-Relationship-Start/dp/1416546464

Dinosaur Wars: Earthfall, by Thomas Hopp

www.amazon.com/Dinosaur-Wars-Earthfall-Thomas-Hopp-ebook/dp/ B004IWQXKW

Amish Vampires in Space, by Kerry Nietz

www.amazon.com/Amish-Vampires-Space-Kerry-Nietz/dp/1940163048

Pack of 6 White Decorative Ceramic Accent Balls 3.5"

www.walmart.com/msharbor/ip/Pack-of-6-White-Decorative-Ceramic-Accent-Balls-3.5/26828794

Fire Dragon Figure

www.toysrus.com/buy/science-fiction-fantasy/fire-dragon-38981-23777746

Chapter 3: What Did You Expect? Dating Edition

Jaguars Club, El Paso, TX

www.ktsm.com/news/shots-fired-bouncers-outside-east-el-paso-strip-club
Photo courtesy of NewsChannel 9 KTSM

Dream-Marriage.com

http://en.wikipedia.org/wiki/Women_in_ the_Russian_and_Soviet_military

U.S. Army, Kabul, Afghanistan

http://commons.wikimedia.org/wiki/ File:Afghanistan_-_American_Soldiers_ FOB_Baylough.jpg
Photo courtesy of Staff Sgt. William Tremblay, U.S. Army

Fatty Patty Blow Up Doll

www.spencersonline.com/product/big-girl-doll/

Chapter 4: Not Their Fault

Laptops for Seniors for Dummies, by Nancy C. Muir

www.barnesandnoble.com/w/laptops-for-seniors-for-dummies-nancy-c-muir/11002 96727?ean=9781118711057

The Godfather Collection: The Coppola Restoration (Blu-ray)

www.amazon.com/Godfather-Collection-Coppola-Restoration-Blu-ray/dp/ B000NTPDSW

Les Misérables (Kindle Edition)
www.amazon.com/Misérables-English-language-Victor-Hugo-ebook/dp/B004GHNIRK

The Lord of the Rings, by J.R.R. Tolkien
www.amazon.com/The-Lord-Rings-Publisher-Mariner/dp/B004N8MT68

Motel 6 Hollywood, Los Angeles, CA
www.motel6.com/reservations/motel_detail.aspx?num=4044

CTA Digital Kitchen Knife Block with Adjustable View iPad Holder
www.smarthome.com/61139/CTA-Digital-PAD-BKS-Kitchen-Knife-Block-with-Adjustable-View-iPad-Holder/p.aspx

Pow Gloves Hiro-Shaka Glove White
www.amazon.com/POW-Hiro-Shaka-Glove-White-Large/dp/B005IEOUAY

Hopscotch Technology BOB The Screentime Controller
www.smarthome.com/7844/Hopscotch-Technology-BOB-The-Screen-Time-Controller/p.aspx

iRobot Roomba 550 Vacuum Cleaning Robot
http://reviews.costco.com/2070/11497668/irobot-irobot-roomba-550-vacuum-cleaning-robot-reviews/reviews.htm

"Tasty Tyrone" Inflatable Doll
www.spencersonline.com/product/tasty-tyrone-inflatable-doll/

Dr. Atkins' New Diet Revolution, Revised Edition, by Robert C. Atkins, MD
www.amazon.com/Atkins-Diet-Revolution-Revised-Edition-ebook/dp/B004HINCLK

Love (German Edition), by Stephen King
www.amazon.de/Love-Stephen-King/dp/3453265327

Sonic Alert SB1000 Sonic Boom Alarm Clock
www.smarthome.com/52366/Sonic-Alert-SB1000-Sonic-Boom-Alarm-Clock/p.aspx

McDreams Hotel, Wuppertal City, Germany
http://nz.hotels.com/ho447724/mcdreams-hotel-wuppertal-city-wuppertal-germany/

My Size Darth Vader Figure
http://tvmoviegifts.com/DarthVaderFigure

Chapter 5: Super Fans and Contrarians

Frozen (2013)
http://disneyaddict.com/2014/02/13/frozens-broadway-beginnings/
Photo courtesy of Walt Disney Pictures

The Lord of the Rings Trilogy, by J.R.R. Tolkien
www.amazon.com/The-Lord-Rings-Publisher-Mariner/dp/B004N8MT68

The Fellowship of the Ring, by J.R.R. Tolkien
www.barnesandnoble.com/w/fellowship-of-the-ring-j-r-r-tolkien/1100013647?ean=9780618346257

Anna Karenina, by Leo Tolstoy
www.jessmountifield.co.uk/2013/07/26/anna-karenina-a-review/

Jurassic Park (1993)
www.loganmauldin.com/2013/05/26/jurassic-park-1993-228/
Photo courtesy of Universal Pictures

Game of Thrones, HBO, 2011–Present
http://metro.co.uk/2014/03/02/the-real-game-of-thrones-game-readers-feature-4344668/
Photo courtesy of HBO

The Shawshank Redemption (1994)
http://filmplicity.com/2012/02/memorable-movie-epithets-if-you-could-have-any-line-from-any-movie-on-your-tombstone-what-would-it-be/
Photo courtesy of Castle Rock Entertainment

Harry Potter and the Half-Blood Prince Bad Group: Collector's Beaded Bookmark
www.amazon.com/Harry-Potter-Half-Blood-Prince-Group/dp/B003MNUUNE

The Hunger Games (2012)
http://collider.com/the-hunger-games-tv-spot/
Photo courtesy of Lionsgate

Expendables Action Figure: Barney Ross
www.amazon.com/Diamond-Select-Expendables-Barney-Action/dp/B00AZ60SQA

Chapter 6: Entitlement A-Go-Go

Subsolo Spanish Restaurant & Bar, Sydney, Australia
www.subsolo.com.au/gallery

Hooters Restaurant, Culpeper, VA
https://plus.google.com/+hooters/photos

Walt Disney World, Orlando, FL
http://commons.wikimedia.org/wiki/File:Cinderella_Castle.jpg
Photo courtesy of Katie Rommel-Esham

Sala Spa Massage, Phuket, Thailand
http://media-cdn.tripadvisor.com/media/photo-s/01/53/8b/4a/no-sex-sign.jpg
Photo courtesy of meesookho

Walmart.com
www.walmart.com/msharbor/ip/Hometrends-Bayard-Flat-Screen-TV-Console/10793964

SkyMall Pull-Up Christmas Tree
www.skymall.com/pull-up-christmas-tree/418384.html

Vroman's Bookstore, Pasadena, CA
www.vromansbookstore.com/contact-us

Cornbread Cafe: Vegan Comfort Food, Eugene, OR
www.yelp.com/biz_photos/cornbread-cafe-eugene - nWfUOLh-GZ5wHS9pLJ1soA
Photo courtesy of Sheree W.

Chapter 7: Don't Add Kids

Good Luck Charlie, Disney Channel
www.broadwayworld.com/bwwtv/article/Disney-Channel-to-Air-Series-Finale-of-GOOD-LUCK-CHARLIE-216-20140214
Photo courtesy of Disney Channel

Sylvan Complete At-Home System: School Success, Ages 8-12
http://pixabay.com/en/child-book-boy-studying-isolated-316510

Better Bedding, Orange, CT
http://sleepysblog.com

Walmart, Liberty, MO
http://commons.wikimedia.org/wiki/File:Walmart-supercentre-canada_129858013133613481.JPG
Photo courtesy of Benchapple

Johnson's Baby Bubble Bath & Wash
www.walmart.com/ip/Johnson-s-Baby-Bubble-Bath-Wash-15-fl-oz/16940619

My Little Pony Nightmare Moon Figure
www.toysrus.com/buy/her-universe/my-little-pony-nightmare-moon-a5100-20324126

Chapter 8: One-Star Products

Mood Finger Scan App by Indigo Penguin Limited
https://itunes.apple.com/us/app/mood-finger-scan/id405862075?mt=8

Hanes Big Men's Flannel Pajama Set
www.walmart.com/ip/Hanes-Big-Men-s-Flannel-Pajama-Set/20975364

Tink's Miss November Doe Decoy
www.walmart.com/ip/Tink-s-Miss-November-Doe-Decoy/14658251

Valhalla Rising (2009)
www.imdb.com/title/tt0862467/
Photo courtesy of BBC Films

Techko S096 Solar Powered Vibration Sensor Entry Alarm
www.smarthome.com/32449/Techko-S096-Solar-Powered-Vibration-Sensor-Entry-Alarm/p.aspx

SQUEELER R/C All Terrain Vehicle
www.hookedontoys.com/productdetails.aspx?ItemID=3270&ParentCatID=194

Thierry Mugler Womanity Eau de Parfum
www.thebeautyoflifeblog.com/2010/07/citizen-of-womanity-thierry-mugler.html

Yatagan Eau de Toilette by Caron
www.perfumeparadise.ca/him/yatagan-by-caron-edt-spray-125ml-detail.html

Just Kidz 18 in. Good Kids Doll
www.kmart.com/just-kidz-18-in-good-kids-doll-brunette/p-004W005372450008P

Miss BIC for Her Medium Ballpoint Pen (Box of 12), Black
www.amazon.com/BIC-MISS-BALLPEN-BLACK-PK12/dp/B004FTGJUW

Smart Border Collie Sticker
www.zazzle.com/smart_border_collie_bumper_sticker-128171593320576392
Photo courtesy of Gwyllion

Veet Fast Acting Gel Cream Hair Remover For Legs & Body
www.ulta.com/ulta/browse/productDetail.jsp?productId=xlsImpprod4200297

Chapter 9: One-Star Restaurants

Colony Cafe, Miami Beach, FL
http://commons.wikimedia.org/wiki/File:Colony_Hotel_Miami.jpg
Photo courtesy of Ad Meskens

Bucatini Restaurant & Bar, Mitcham, Australia
www.tripadvisor.com/Restaurant_Review-g154982-d5073428-Reviews-Bucatini_Restaurant_Wine_Bar-Brampton_Ontario.html
Photo courtesy of Bucatini Restaurant & Bar

Blundell Arms, Horwich, United Kingdom
www.geograph.org.uk/photo/107028
Photo courtesy of Margaret Clough

Soprano Cafe & Italian Restaurant, Miami Beach, FL
http://media-cdn.tripadvisor.com/media/photo-s/01/28/90/4a/miami-beach.jpg
Photo courtesy of MiamiMartin77

Chapter 10: One-Star Hotels

Club Aqua Gumbet Hotel, Gumbet, Turkey
http://media-cdn.tripadvisor.com/media/photo-o/03/77/70/aa/view.jpg
Photo courtesy of BInspiredBeauty

Hotel Erwin, Venice Beach, CA
www.kicksonfire.com/2012/12/10/kicks-diary-kobe-bryant-launches-the-nike-kobe-8-system-in-venice-beach
Photo courtesy of Juan Martinez

Travelodge Palm Springs, Palm Springs, CA
www.tripadvisor.com/Hotel_Review-g186338-d597383-Reviews-Travelodge_Wembley-London_England.html - 79303054P
hoto courtesy of Travelodge

Chapter 11: One-Star Books

Secret Sins, **by Lora Leigh**
www.kupindo.com/Knjige-na-engleskom-jeziku/14853161_Secret-Sins-By-Lora-Leigh

Breaking Dawn **by Stephenie Meyer**
www.amazon.com/Breaking-Dawn-Twilight-Saga-Book/dp/0316067938/

The Blonde Geisha, **by Jina Bacarr**
www.prweb.com/releases/2006Blonde/7Geisha/prweb412288.htm

Naked Sushi, **by Jina Bacarr**
http://goodbooksandgoodwine.com/2013/08/naked-sushi-jina-bacarr-novella-review.html

Eternal Pleasure, **by Nina Bangs**
www.badlandgirls.com/2012/09/episode-34-darkly-erotic-punch.html

Zombie Rain, **by Zach Sweets**
www.goodreads.com/book/show/13124539-zombie-rain

Pleasuring the Pirate, **by Emily Bryan**
http://suchabooknerd.wordpress.com/2011/02/09/smut-ahoy-matey-pleasuring-the-pirate-by-emily-bryan/

Moon People, **by Dale M. Courtney**
www.amazon.com/Moon-People-Dale-M-Courtney/dp/1436372135

Midnight Sins, **by Lora Leigh**
www.amazon.com/Midnight-Sins-Lora-Leigh/dp/0312389086/

A Taint in the Blood, **by S.M. Stirling**
www.openlettersmonthly.com/book-review-a-taint-in-the-blood/

The 2009-2014 World Outlook for 60-Milligram Containers of Fromage Frais, **by Professor Philip M. Parker, PhD**
www.amazon.com/2009-2014-Outlook-60-Milligram-Containers-Fromage/dp/0497929503

Hitler: Neither Vegetarian Nor Animal Lover, **by Rynn Berry**
www.oddee.com/item_96894.aspx

The Salaryman's Wife, **by Sujata Massey**
www.goodreads.com/book/show/412242.The_Salaryman_s_Wife

The Big Book of Lesbian Horse Stories, **by Alisa Surkis and Monica Nolan**
www.amazon.ca/The-Book-Lesbian-Horse-Stories-ebook/dp/B008J4N9FC

Bombproof Your Horse: Teach Your Horse to Be Confident, Obedient, and Safe, No Matter What You Encounter, **by Rick Pelicano**
www.amazon.com/Bombproof-Your-Horse-Confident-Encounter/dp/1570762600

Chapter 12: The Unsorted

Uranium Ore
www.amazon.com/Images-SI-Uranium-Ore/dp/B000796XXM

Samsung UN85S9 85-Inch 4K Ultra HD 120Hz 3D Smart LED Television
www.abt.com/product/69497/Samsung-UN85S9AFXZA.html

Yodok Concentration Camp, Yodok County, South Hamgyong Province, North Korea
http://commons.wikimedia.org/wiki/File:JointSecurityAreaNorthKoreans.jpg
Photo courtesy of Edward N. Johnson

Area 51, Nevada
http://commons.wikimedia.org/wiki/File:Wfm_x51_area51_warningsign.jpg
Photo courtesy of X51

Mount Everest, Nepal
http://commons.wikimedia.org/wiki/File:Mt._Everest_from_Gokyo_Ri_November_5,_2012.jpg
Photo courtesy of Rdevany

The United States Army
http://commons.wikimedia.org/wiki/File:Flickr_-_The_U.S._Army_-_www.Army.mil_%28262%29.jpg
Photo courtesy of The United States Army

Leonardo DiCaprio
http://commons.wikimedia.org/wiki/File:Leonardo_DiCaprio_2010.jpg
Photo courtesy of Siebbi

Gerbils
http://commons.wikimedia.org/wiki/File:Meriones_unguiculatus_%28wild%29.jpg
Photo courtesy of Alastair Rae

Fascism
http://commons.wikimedia.org/wiki/File:Benito_Mussolini_and_Adolf_Hitler.jpg
Photo courtesy of Muzej Revolucije Narodnosti Jugoslavije

Astronauts
http://commons.wikimedia.org/wiki/File:Astronaut_Mike_Hopkins_on_Dec._24_Spacewalk.jpg
Photo courtesy of NASA